D1550391

THE SIMON AND SCHUSTER

BOOK OF

FACTS

AND

FALLACIES

THE SIMON AND SCHUSTER
BOOK OF
FACTS
AND
FALLACIES

BY
RHODA AND LEDA BLUMBERG

Illustrated by Paul Frame

JULIAN MESSNER
Published by Simon and Schuster, Inc., New York

Copyright © 1983 by Julian Messner
A Division of Simon & Schuster, Inc.
All rights reserved
including the right of reproduction
in whole or in part in any form
Published by JULIAN MESSNER
A Division of
Simon & Schuster, Inc.
Simon & Schuster Building
1230 Avenue of the Americas
New York, New York 10020

Designed by Stanley S. Drate

Manufactured in the United States of America

10 9 8 7 6 5 4 3 2

Julian Messner and colophon are trademarks
of Simon & Schuster, Inc.

Library of Congress Cataloging in Publication Data

Blumberg, Rhoda.
   The Simon and Schuster book of facts and fallacies.

   Includes index.
   Summary: Lays to rest commonly accepted "facts," myths,
and old wives' tales on a variety of topics, including
mammals, American history, inventions, health, food and
drink, sports, and weather.
   1. Errors, Popular—Juvenile literature. [1. Errors,
Popular. 2. Curiosities and wonders] I. Blumberg,
Leda. II. Title.
AZ999.B57 1983   001.9′6   83-6697
ISBN 0-671-47612-2

Also available in Wanderer Edition

FOR TOM AND JERRY

CONTENTS

MAMMALS   9

BIRDS   27

REPTILES, AMPHIBIANS, AND SEA
    CREATURES   35

INSECTS   49

PLANTS   57

AMERICAN AND EUROPEAN
    HISTORY   67

INVENTIONS   85

HEALTH   91

FOOD AND DRINK   99

YOUR MIND AND BODY   109

SPORTS   119

WEATHER   129

LAND, SEA, AND SKY   137

INDEX   155

ABOUT THE AUTHORS   160

MAMMALS

The lion is king of the jungle

The lion is not king of the jungle. In fact, the beast is not even a jungle dweller. A lion lives in open bush and grassy plains, never in a jungle.

Gorillas are dangerous

Despite their huge size, fierce-looking appearance, loud roars, and vigorous chest-beating, gorillas are really gentle, shy, and peace-loving. They live in friendly family groups, and rarely fight with each other. Most of their time is spent gathering and eating plants. When not looking for food, they usually relax and lie in the sun. By beating their chests they warn enemies to keep away. Gorillas also use the loud booming noise of chest-beating to locate other gorillas, especially when they become scattered in their search for food. Gorillas look like strong, hairy humanlike monsters, but they are really gentle giants.

People are the only tool-making animals

Chimpanzees monkey around and make tools, too. They strip leaves from stems and use the stems to take termites from termite nests. The clever chimps also make sponges by chewing leaves. They sop up water from deep tree holes that they can't get their mouths into, by dipping the mashed leaves to sponge up the water. Some monkeys use leaves to pick up seeds and fruit, and use bones to crack nuts.

In addition to certain monkeys and apes, a few birds use tools. The remarkable woodpecker finch breaks off the spine of a cactus, holds it in its beak, and uses it to find insects burrowed in tree bark.

MAMMALS

The California sea otter is another tool user. It picks up rocks in order to smash hard-shelled sea creatures that make up most of its diet. Floating belly up, the otter uses its chest as a table as it bangs away at a shell, then feeds itself with its paws.

The kangaroo is the only animal with a pouch

The kangaroo is only one kind of animal with a pouch. Opossums, koala bears, wombats, and kangaroo rats are some of the many pouched animals (marsupials) on our planet.

Hyenas always eat prey killed by other animals

Hyenas are expert hunters, able to run down and kill large wildebeests and zebras. In many parts of East Africa, hyenas do most of the hunting, and lions do most of the scavenging.

Scavengers feed on flesh killed by other animals. Perhaps the reason hyenas have been called scavengers is that lions sometimes push hyenas away from their kills and force them to wait until after the "king of beasts" has had the lion's share.

White elephants can be found in Asia

So-called white elephants are light gray with pink blotches on their bodies. Their eyes are usually pink, their toenails white, and some tail hairs white. These "white" elephants are albinos. They lack skin pigment. In Thailand they are considered sacred, and are always given to the king.

Elephants are afraid of mice

What an amusing picture: a great big elephant frightened by a tiny mouse! Not so in real life. Elephants fear human beings and big cats, such as leopards and tigers, but they aren't scared silly by a small rodent. In fact, they have been seen inspecting mice with their trunks, then stomping them underfoot.

Elephants drink through their trunks

The trunk looks like a vacuum hose, but an elephant would no more drink water using its trunk than you would by using your nose. An elephant sucks water into its trunk, and then sprays it into its mouth. When bathing, it uses its trunk as a spray shower.

Elephants have their own graveyards

Because hunters found areas with a large number of elephant bones, they believed that elephants went to a special place to die. Ele-

phants are intelligent animals, but they don't choose their graveyards. Areas containing a large quantity of their bones usually mean that a herd died from disease, poisoned water, or starvation.

Beavers use their tails to make dams

The idea that beavers carry and smear mud with their tails is fairy-tale fiction. Beavers carry mud and sticks for dam-building with their front paws. Their tails act as rudders when they swim and are also used to sound warning signals to other beavers. Slapped against the surface of the water, a beaver tail makes a loud splash that can be heard half a mile away.

Beavers fell trees so that they fall toward the water

Although they gnaw down trees, they can't figure out the direction the trees will fall. In many cases beavers are killed by the trees they cut down.

All animals drink water

All animals need water, but some never drink. A few kinds of lizards meet this need by absorbing water through the pores of their skin. Kangaroo rats and jerboas are desert-dwelling rodents that obtain their water from dew-soaked and moisture-filled plants. They survive without drinking. And they don't need water for bathing. They give themselves dust baths.

Big animals give birth to big babies

The size of the baby at birth is not always related to the size of the mother. North American black bears are born small. The cub of a 300-pound mother may weigh less than half a pound. Female kangaroos weigh 60,000 times as much as their newborn bean-sized babies, which measure about one inch (2.54 cm) and weigh less than 1/20th of an ounce (1.42 grams).

Horns and antlers are the same

Many kinds of hooved mammals have horns or antlers for self-protection and for fighting over mates. Although horns and antlers serve the same purpose, they are really quite different. Horns have a bony core, while antlers are made of a hardened skin material. Horns grow throughout an animal's entire life, but antlers are shed and a new pair is grown every year. Many antlers form branches as they grow. Although horns come in a wide variety of shapes (some are spiraled, curved, ridged, or spiked), they never branch.

Horns are worn by antelopes, goats, sheep, and cattle. Members of the deer family, such as whitetails, moose, and caribou, have antlers. Rhinoceros horns aren't true horns, but are a type of modified hair.

Bats are blind

Bats aren't blind. Although they can see, most bats rely on hearing to guide themselves. They send out high-pitched sounds that strike objects and bounce back as echoes. Bats use these echoes to locate things around them. They can fly through dense forests in the dark and not hit a single branch. If blindfolded, they can still fly around without bumping into anything.

MAMMALS

Bats get caught in people's hair	This is an old superstition. Bats don't land on heads. They avoid people and don't hurt them unless they are disturbed. Then they may bite, but they won't tangle with hair.
Vampire bats suck blood	The vampire bat of Central and South America doesn't resemble the dreaded Dracula batman monster. The real vampire is just a few inches long, and although it drinks blood, it doesn't suck blood. It sips it. After biting its victim, it laps up the blood like a kitten drinking milk. And it barely takes more than a teaspoonful. The common vampire bat usually bites a human on the nose or on the big toe! It's not a pain in the neck. The real danger is that its bite can cause rabies.
Camels store water in their humps	The hump is not a water tank. It's made up of fat. The fat nourishes the camel when there is no food or water available. A camel can go for three or four months without drinking. Instead, it digests the fat in the hump. The fat contains liquid.
Lemmings commit suicide by drowning	Lemmings don't rush to water to commit suicide. When they migrate, thousands of them cross streams and lakes. Sometimes they swim out to sea. They don't deliberately enter the ocean in order to drown. Perhaps they mistake the sea for another body of water that must be crossed during their migration. Lemmings are excellent swimmers, but they aren't strong enough to swim across an ocean, a body of water too large for them to cross.

Raccoons wash their food

Raccoons never wash anything. In captivity, raccoons have been seen dipping their food in water. Scientist believe they do this because they are accustomed, when living in the wild, to scooping snails, mussels, and other shelled creatures from the water's edge. When captive, they go through the motion of grabbing prey in the water.

All monkeys live in warm climates

Troops of monkeys can be found high in Asia's snow-covered Himalayas and on the icy peaks of North Africa's Atlas Mountains.

Hippopotamuses sweat blood

During warm weather, the skin of hippopotamuses secretes a reddish, oily fluid that looks like blood. The fluid, known as *pink sweat*, acts as a skin conditioner. It keeps the hippo's thick hide from drying out and cracking when the animal is out of water. Pink sweat isn't blood, and has no blood in it.

Opossums "play dead"

The common expression *playing possum* means faking death. Many opossums faced with danger fall over with their mouths open, their tongues hanging out, their eyes partly closed, and their heartbeats slowed down. Seemingly dead, they will not stir, even if they are swung by their tales.

However, they are not deliberately playing dead. They fall into a trance caused by fear. They can't control this reaction. Enemies lose interest in seemingly dead opossums and leave them alone.

MAMMALS

Many opossums don't react to danger by "playing possum." When threatened, they hiss and snap, run away, or climb a tree.

Opossums hang from their tails

The widespread belief that opossums hang from their tails and sleep in this position is false. Tails can't support their full weight. Opossums use their hairless tails for balancing and supporting themselves as they climb trees.

Porcupines shoot their quills

Porcupines don't throw their quills, but occasionally quills fly off when they slap their tails from side to side. When threatened by another animal, porcupines raise their quills, back into their enemy, and lash their tails from side to side. The quills don't shoot out, but they have hooked barbs that easily come off and stick to any animal that touches them. Porcupines can drive off almost any animal, even one as large as a bear, because of their needle-sharp quills.

Skunks spray with their tails

The smelly spray comes from a gland beneath the tail, not from the tail itself. Peaceful by nature, skunks usually don't spray unless they're frightened. Even then, they usually warn their enemies first before spraying. They stamp their feet. If this doesn't frighten their foe, they turn their backs, raise their tails, and squirt a yellow smelly fluid. They can aim this fluid accurately as far as twelve feet (3.66 meters). The spray not only smells bad, it causes choking, and if it gets into an animal's eyes, it stings and causes temporary blindness.

Cats see in the dark	Cats can see better than humans when the light is poor. However, no animal can see in complete darkness. In a photographer's darkroom, a cat wouldn't see any better than you do.
All cats have hair	One breed, the Sphinx, is hairless, and doesn't even have whiskers.
If you starve a cat, it will kill more mice	This false belief has caused many cats to be underfed. Cats are natural hunters. They stalk prey whenever they can, hungry or not. Well-fed cats are healthier and stronger, and therefore more likely to catch mice, moles, and other small creatures.
All cats hate water	Many cats aren't fond of water, but some, like Abyssinian cats, enjoy playing in water and swimming. Tigers, one of the largest members of the cat family, are strong swimmers, swimming to cool off in hot weather and to cross rivers.
Falling cats always land on their feet	Although cats are extremely agile acrobats, able to twist their bodies around in midair, their is no guarantee that they'll land on their feet when they fall. Many cats have been severely injured when they fell from high places. Be careful with your pet cat. It doesn't really have nine lives!

MAMMALS

All rodents are small

Not only rats and mice, but squirrels, chipmunks, woodchucks, and prairie dogs are rodents. All these are midgets compared with the capybara, an animal of Central and South America, that can be four feet long (1.22 m) and weigh 150 pounds (68.04 kg). Because it lives near rivers and streams, and is an excellent swimmer, this giant rodent is also called a water hog.

Mice are quiet animals

The expression *quiet as a mouse* is quite common, but these little critters are noisy. In addition to squeaking, mice twitter, chirp, and warble.

Mice love cheese

Despite all the cartoons you have seen of mice nibbling cheese, cheese is not their favorite food. They prefer seeds, nuts, and fresh vegetables.

Dogs sweat through their tongues

A dog sticks out its tongue to cool off, not because it is sweating. Dogs have sweat glands on their bodies, especially on the soles of their feet.

Healthy dogs have cold, wet noses

No nose lets you know a dog's state of health. A healthy dog can have a cold and wet, warm and dry, warm and wet, or cold and dry snout, and still be healthy.

Goats eat tin cans

They eat a wide variety of foods, but tin cans aren't part of their diet. Goats have a taste for glue. Therefore, they seem to be eating tin cans when they are actually chewing for the glue under a label. No kidding!

Pigs are dirty animals

Hogwash! Pigs don't have sweat glands to cool them. They are thick-skinned and get hot easily. In order to cool off, pigs wallow in mud—or bathe in water. They wallow in muck only if there isn't a cleaner way to cool off.

Pigs are thought of as disgusting because they eat garbage, but that is what they are often fed by their owners.

Bulls attack when they see red

Bulls can't see red. They're color-blind. It isn't the color of a bullfighter's cape that makes a bull mad. It's having a cape waved around in front of him, plus the noise of a cheering crowd that infuriates him. Mammals, with the exception of humans, most other primates, and possibly a few other species, are color-blind.

Moles don't have eyes

Although their vision is quite poor, moles do have eyes. Most moles are able to distinguish light from dark. Their eyes may be covered with skin or buried in fur. You may not see their eyes, but they are there.

Rabbits should be lifted by their ears

Never! Rabbits' ears are not handles. They are very delicate and will injure easily. The best way to lift a rabbit is by grasping the loose skin above its shoulders and supporting its body with your other arm.

MAMMALS

Flying squirrels fly

Flying squirrels should really be called gliding squirrels! The so-called wings of flying squirrels are not true wings, but are flaps of skin attaching the front and hind legs. By spreading these flaps, flying squirrels can glide through the air when leaping from tree to tree. Bats are the only mammals that can truly fly.

Rabbits and hares are the same

Although there are many similarities, rabbits and hares are not the same. Hares are born furry and with their eyes open. Rabbit babies are born blind, hairless, and helpless. Rabbits live in groups in underground burrows, called *warrens*, while hares live alone in simple above-ground nests.

Here are some confusing facts: jackrabbits and snowshoe rabbits are actually hares, and the Belgian hare is really a rabbit!

Groundhogs can foretell the coming of spring

In America, February 2 is Groundhog Day. Groundhogs supposedly come out of their burrows. If it's sunny and they see their shadows, there will be six more weeks of winter. If it's a cloudy day, and there's no shadow, spring will be early that year.

Groundhogs aren't weather forecasters. And they aren't hogs. They are woodchucks.

Squirrels hoard more nuts before a severe winter

Squirrels hoard as many nuts as they can before winter, but they can't foretell future weather. If they could, weather forecasters would be counting nuts that squirrels collected, and we would be able to know what kind of winter to expect. Instead, all anyone can learn from the squirrel's activities would be whether or not it was a good nut-collecting season.

Prairie dogs are dogs

Prairie dogs aren't dogs. These short-tailed rodents are members of the squirrel family. They received their name because they live on prairies and they bark like dogs.

Koala bears are bears

Although they resemble bears, Australia's koalas are not bears; they're marsupials. Like kangaroos, the females have pouches in which they raise their young. Mother koalas carry their young in their pouches for about six months, then on their backs for another six months.

Koalas have various names: Australian teddy bear, koolewang, bagaroo, cullawino, and buidelbeer!

Panda bears are bears

Scientists are still debating where panda bears fit into animal classification. All agree that they are not bears. Physically they are more like raccoons.

Pandas are probably in a class by themselves.

Black bears are black

Black bears range in color from light brown to black; and in some northern regions they can be a gray or off-white.

Guinea pigs are pigs from Guinea

Guinea pigs aren't pigs, and they don't come from Guinea! They are plump rodents that originally came from South America, where the Inca Indians of Peru raised them for food and kept them as pets.

European traders brought the first guinea pigs across the Atlantic from South America. These traders were called "guineamen" by English-speaking people, which probably accounts for the name *guinea pig*. Some people call guinea pigs *cavies*, their native Peruvian name.

A ten-year-old horse is old

At age ten, many horses are just reaching their prime. Many Olympic-caliber horses are well into their teens when they compete internationally. A horse's life expectancy averages about thirty years, but several have lived into their forties. The thoroughbred racehorse Tango Duke was forty-two years old when he died in 1978.

Horses sleep standing up

Horses can drowse while standing up, but they must lie down to go into a true deep sleep. Most horses lie down and get up several times a night.

MAMMALS

Young horses are born with adult-sized legs

Although young horses are born with long, gangly legs, their legs continue to grow until they reach their full height, usually after three years.

Purebred horses are thoroughbreds

Not all purebred horses are thoroughbreds. A purebred horse has ancestors that come from the same breed or kind. For example, a Clydesdale, an Arabian, or a Morgan horse can be a purebred. A thoroughbred horse is just another breed of horse that was developed in England during the eighteenth century.

Lame horses are always shot

Because horses are big, heavy animals on long, thin legs, lameness is common. Most leg problems can be treated, and rarely require that horses be "put down" or shot. Even horses with fractures have been treated and used for riding or breeding.

Males are always the leaders in the animal world

This may shock the male chauvinists: females often rule, and the males play "second fiddle." The oldest, strongest female elephants are queens of the herd. The males, called bulls, are forced to keep their distance from the queens and from their princess daughters—except during mating season. Hyenas, lemurs, and caribous also have female bosses. Among the birds, female snow buntings, boobies, and ravens rule the roosts. And in the insect world the queen bee, wasp, and termite reign supreme. The males are merely tolerated for mating, and after that they die.

BIRDS

All birds build nests

This statement is strictly for the birds. Although many nest, some live in tree holes. Others make their homes on sand or grass, or on stone cliffs. Some birds are tricksters that use nests belonging to other birds. Cowbirds and cuckoos, for example, not only lay their eggs in other birds' nests, but they allow the actual nest owners to hatch and raise their young. King and Emperor penguins are the only birds that don't even need a nesting site. They carry their eggs about on their feet. A fold of skin over the foot protects the egg (always one) from extreme cold.

Birds sleep with their heads under their wings

When birds sleep, they usually turn their heads around and place their beaks on their backs, not under their wings. The beaks often become buried under feathers.

BIRDS

Fallen baby birds can't be returned to their nests

Fallen baby birds can successfully be returned to their nests. However, never tamper with a bird's nest or the parents may abandon it.

All birds fly

All birds have wings, but about fifty kinds of birds don't fly. Ostriches, the largest of birds, can't fly. They escape their enemies by outrunning them, and sometimes speed ahead at forty miles per hour (64.37 km). Their wings help them balance and turn. Penguins, also flightless birds, use their long, flipperlike wings as swimming paddles. Cassowaries, emus, rheas, and kiwis are other flightless birds.

Some birds became extinct because they couldn't fly. The dodo, for example, waddled about on islands in the Indian Ocean until sailors arrived and knocked the birds over with clubs. The last dodo died in 1681.

Birds can only fly forwards

Hummingbirds can fly forwards, backwards, sideways, straight up, down, and can hover in one spot. The wings of these tiny birds beat so fast (fifty to eighty times per second) that they appear as a blur.

Ostriches stick their heads in the sand

For thousands of years, ostriches have been symbols of stupidity. They supposedly think they can't be seen if they hide their heads in the sand. This is not true. Occasionally, ostriches poke their heads in the sand, but it is to find underground drinking water, not to hide. When they see enemies, they either run away, lie down and hide, or fight by kicking, hissing and pecking. Their strong legs enable them to outrace many enemies, and give them powerful kicks. Ostriches hide by crouching on the sand, their necks stretched flat against the ground. In this position, their loose feathers make them look like bushes. That's not stupid!

Ostriches eat anything, even coins and keys

Like many other birds, ostriches must swallow grit, gravel, or sand to help digest their food. Because they lack teeth, they use grit to grind food inside their stomachs. In captivity, ostriches may swallow almost any small objects that are offered to them, even coins and keys. But these metal objects are not digested, and can make them sick.

Only female birds incubate eggs

There are many "brooding fathers" in the bird world. Scientists estimate that in more than half the bird families both sexes share the task of caring for eggs. In many cases, only the male is in charge of his future offspring. Female phalaropes and button quails, for example, choose mates, lay eggs, and then leave the scene. The males are left with the job of incubating and hatching the eggs. Even when the young emerge, the fathers are in charge.

A hen cannot lay an egg without being near a rooster

Hens don't need roosters in order to lay eggs. The eggs, however, won't hatch into chicks unless a rooster mates with a hen and makes the eggs fertile. Most of the eggs we eat are from roosterless henhouses.

 BIRDS

Birds can foretell weather conditions	If that were so, why do so many birds fly directly into bad weather that causes their death or injury?
Bald eagles are bald	They don't have hair on their heads, but there are plenty of feathers. They appear to be bald because their snow-white head and neck feathers contrast with the brown feathers on the rest of the body. Until they are seven years old, young bald eagles have dark feathers on their heads as well as over their bodies.
Scarecrows frighten birds because they resemble people	Birds are scared away because of the smell, not the sight, of scarecrows. The clothing on scarecrows has the odor of a human being, and that turns the birds away. When scarecrows have been exposed to a lot of wind and rain, the smell wears off, and the birds might even perch on them.
Crows always fly in a straight line	You've heard the expression *as straight as the crow flies*. Although they can fly in a straight line, crows often zigzag across the sky.
The loon is a crazy bird	A loon is a North American water bird known for its strange, laughing call that carries great distances. There's nothing crazy or "loony" about that. The expression *crazy as a loon* is not for the birds.

Owls are blind in the daylight

The notion that owls can't see in daylight is widespread but untrue. Owls have excellent vision in daylight. In complete darkness they are as blind as we humans. However, they are able to see better than we do in dim light. Although most owls hunt at night, some kinds hunt during the day. Their eyes are keen enough to recognize colors. When examining an object, an owl can swivel its head around almost 180 degrees, so that its head seem to be on backwards.

Penguins live at the North Pole

You're heading in the wrong direction if you travel north in order to find penguin country. Penguins live at the South Pole, and in the cold seas of South Africa, South America, Australia, and New Zealand.

A robin's presence is the first sign of spring

Spring may be the first time *we* notice them, but many robins spend the entire winter as far north as New England. During the extremely cold weather these birds aren't easily spotted, for they stay in forests.

The American robin belongs to the thrush family. The European robin redbreast, a different kind of bird, also can be seen when the snow falls.

Robins listen for worms

A robin hopping around cocking its head from side to side and plucking worms from the earth is looking, not listening, for worms. Because its eyes are on the sides of its head, a robin must tilt its head to see worms.

BIRDS

The Canary Islands were named after canary birds

The opposite is true. Canaries were named for the islands on which they were originally found. The islands got their name from the Latin word *canis*, meaning "dog," because there were many large dogs (canines) living there.

Blackbirds are black

Of the close to 100 kinds of blackbirds, many aren't black. And, many black-colored birds aren't blackbirds! Most female blackbirds are gray. Some of the more common blackbirds are orioles, grackles, cowbirds, yellow-headed blackbirds, and red-winged blackbirds.

Birds don't fly higher than one thousand feet

Radar has shown that most migrating birds fly so high that we can't see them from the ground. Geese, storks, and cranes can fly four miles (over 20,000 feet) (6.44 km) up, and go over the Himalayan Mountains.

Airplane pilots are well aware of the heights to which birds ascend. They must avoid midair collisions with creatures on the wing. Whistling swans have winged their way 4,000 feet (1,219.2 m) high in the sky. Blue geese can travel a mile (1.61 km) up. Mallard ducks have been seen four miles (6.44 km) up.

Reptiles, Amphibians, and Sea Creatures

Dinosaurs are the largest animals that ever lived

The great blue whale is the largest animal that ever lived. The *Brachiosaurus*, the largest dinosaur that roamed the earth millions of years ago, weighed over 75 tons (68,040 kilos) and was over 70 feet long (21.34 m). A blue whale can weigh as much as 150 tons (136,080 kilos) and measure 100 feet (30.48m). This giant swims the world's oceans today.

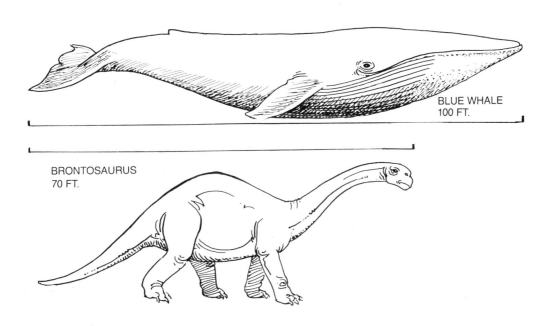

BLUE WHALE
100 FT.

BRONTOSAURUS
70 FT.

All dinosaurs were huge

The word *dinosaur* means "fearfully great" in Greek. But some of these prehistoric reptiles were small. The *Compsognathus dinosaur* when full grown was no bigger than a turkey. Its fossil remains were found in Germany.

REPTILES, AMPHIBIANS, AND SEA CREATURES

Cave men saw dinosaurs

The real Fred Flintstones never saw these giant reptiles. Dinosaurs roamed the earth more than 50 million years before human beings became part of the animal kingdom.

Fossils are bones of extinct animals

Fossils are not necessarily bones. They can be any remains, traces, or impressions of plants or animals that once lived. Footprints as well as bones of dinosaurs are fossils. Fossils may be oak leaves, seaweeds, worms, horses, clams, and insects, as well as dinosaurs, mammoths, and prehistoric sharks.

Most fossils are *petrified*, or turned to stone. Some are frozen in arctic swamps, preserved in a natural deep-freeze. Many animals walked into pools of tar and sank. Their bones, preserved for thousands of years, became fossils. Insects and flowers have been preserved in amber. Amber is hardened tree sap.

Poisonous snakes always have pointed heads

It's true that pit vipers, rattlers, copperheads, and many other poisonous fang-bearers have pointed heads. However, cobras and coral snakes don't have pointed heads, and you wouldn't want to step on them. Also, many nonpoisonous snakes have large, pointed triangular heads.

There's one sure way of identifying a poisonous snake. There are two long fangs on its upper jaw. A nonvenomous snake doesn't have fangs. The best advice is not to look too closely.

Snakes feel slimy	Their skin usually feels very dry. Snake scales often look wet when the sunlight makes them shine.
Snakes are dangerous	Although many people think of snakes as evil and dangerous creatures, most of the more than 2,000 species are harmless, timid, and avoid people. Most farmers welcome snakes because they eat rats and mice, and therefore help keep down the ever-expanding rodent population.
Snakes always coil before striking	Snakes usually warn enemies before striking. Some rattle their tails, others hiss or coil. However, there are snakes that strike out with no warning at all. Watch your step!
Some snakes swallow their young to protect them	It's true that some big snakes will swallow small snakes, but it isn't to protect them, but to make a meal of them. Some snakes even eat their own offspring.
Some snakes sway to music	In many parts of Asia and Africa, snake charmers make their living by playing flutes or other wind instruments and having poisonous snakes sway to the rhythms of their music. But snakes don't have an ear for music. In fact, they don't have ears. They respond to motions made by the snake charmer, not to sounds. When the charmer sways, the snake, eyeing its owner, sways also. The tunes and commands of the charmer are for the audience.

REPTILES, AMPHIBIANS, AND SEA CREATURES

By counting the number of rattles, you can find out the age of a rattlesnake

A rattle, which is a loose piece of skin, is usually added to the tail each time the snake sheds its skin. The number of times a rattler sheds depends upon the amount of food it eats. It may not shed its skin one year, then shed three times another year. In zoos these North American noisemakers may have as many as twenty-nine rattles. In the wild, rattlers seldom have more than fourteen, because their tails rub against hard objects and wear down. Should you see one in the fields, don't start counting. Get away! Rattlers don't always shake their tails before striking.

Glass snakes are snakes

The glass snake is really a legless lizard that looks and moves like a snake. Because it has movable eyelids and has ears, it is classified as a lizard. Snakes don't have ears or movable eyelids.

Milk snakes like cow's milk

Cow barns have grain for cows to eat. Grain attracts rodents, like rats and mice. Rodents attract milk snakes that dine on them. Occasionally, farmers find milk snakes inside their barns, but the snakes are helping themselves to rodents, not milk.

Boa constrictors crush their victims to death

Boas don't crush their victims. They cause them to stop breathing. Boa constrictors kill by coiling themselves around their victims and tightening their coils so that the victim can't breathe, and dies. Many other snakes, like king snakes, corn snakes, and rat snakes, use this method to kill prey.

Hog-nosed snakes are dangerous

A frightened hog-nosed snake may look scary, but it's really quite harmless. It may raise the front of its body, puff up its neck like a cobra, hiss, and pretend to strike. This fearsome display is an act designed to scare enemies away. If the hog-nose fails to scare its enemy, it performs its other act: flopping over on its back and playing dead.

Snakes will not cross a horsehair rope

Campers who encircle their sleeping bags with horsehair ropes aren't protecting themselves against snakes, though they may think they are. Ropes of any kind can't keep snakes away. It's not the ropes but the people that snakes usually avoid. If snakes knew how to rope us off, they would do so.

You can get warts from touching toads

Handling toads won't give you warts, but it can cause other problems. All toads have protective glands on both sides of their heads. These produce a thick, poisonous mucus. Getting this mucus on your hands won't hurt you, but if you rub your eyes or put your fingers in your mouth, you'll feel an unpleasant burning sensation.

If a dog eats a toad, the mucus sticks in the dog's throat and stomach, making the dog sick. In some cases, animals that eat toads die from the poison.

Horned toads are toads

Horned toads are not toads. They are lizards with toadlike faces. They have broad flat bodies and "horns," which are really sharp

REPTILES, AMPHIBIANS, AND SEA CREATURES

scales. These bristle out of their heads and bodies.

There are more than a dozen kinds of horned toads in North America. When frightened, some spurt blood from their eyes from a distance of up to three feet (91.44 cm).

Crocodiles live to be several hundred years old

Audiences at reptile shows in various parts of the world are often told that the crocodiles they are looking at are hundreds of years old. That's show-business talk, not scientific information. Crocodiles are not known to live more than fifty years.

Chameleons change color to match their surroundings

A chameleon placed on a red cloth doesn't turn red. It doesn't turn green if placed on the grass. And it won't have a nervous breakdown if it crawls on plaid. Of the sixteen kinds of chameleon lizards, several blend naturally with their surroundings. Some have brown skin that matches the color of tree bark. Others are as green as plant leaves.

Chameleons do have the remarkable ability to change color. However, this usually has nothing to do with their surroundings. Temperature, light, and the creature's emotions cause color change. Some angry chameleons go black with rage. Others display greenish skin with yellow polka dots when they're excited.

Fish can't drown

They can! Like all animals, fish must breathe oxygen to stay alive. Their gills take oxygen from water. But if a fish swims in water that can't supply enough oxygen, it must swim to another area, or drown. Millions of fish drown each year as a result of pollution that destroys the oxygen supplies in waters.

An octopus can strangle a man

Rather than tangle with swimmers and deep-sea divers, octopuses retreat. They often hide behind rocks and in holes, or change color so that they blend with their surroundings. They might squirt "ink" to keep people away.

Octopuses don't squeeze other sea creatures to death. Their eight arms are used to hold their victims as they bite with their hard, parrotlike beaks.

All fish lay eggs

Many kinds of fish, including guppies, surfperches, most sharks, and all skates don't lay eggs, but give birth to live young. The offspring hatch when the eggs are inside the body of the mother. The shells are soft and are eventually expelled.

Fish can't live out of water

Anyone who believes that fish story hasn't learned about climbing perch, mudskippers, lungfish, and assorted varieties of other finned creatures.

REPTILES, AMPHIBIANS, AND SEA CREATURES

India's climbing perch can travel many miles over land by wriggling about. They carry their water supply in pockets inside their heads. Far more expert as land rovers are the mudskippers of Africa. These fish climb trees and leap from branch to branch in search of tasty insects. Their front fins act as feet, and they breathe air through their gills. African lungfish also become land creatures. When swamps and streams dry up they burrow in mud, where they can survive for more than one year, even when the mud becomes dry and hard as a rock.

Sharks are dangerous man-eaters

Of the approximately 300 species of sharks, only a few have attacked humans. These are the great white shark, the tiger shark, the blue shark, and the hammerhead. Bulls, snakes, and spiders kill more people than do sharks.

Flying fish fly

Flying fish are small, silvery fish that appear to fly above the ocean's waves. They can speed above the water at forty-five miles per hour (72.4 kmph) and their "flights" can be hundreds of feet long. In most cases, however, these long "flights" are made up of many separate flights lasting eight to fifteen seconds each.

Moreover, they don't fly, they glide on the surface of the water. Flying fish vibrate their tails to gain speed. Then they spread their large, winglike front fins and glide through the air. In that way they escape enemy sea creatures.

Crab shells found on beaches are the remains of dead crabs

While walking along the beach, you may find some old crab shells. Occasionally, these are the remains of dead crabs. In most cases, they are shells that were shed by crabs who outgrow their hard cases and must grow new shells to fit their expanding bodies. Like snakes shedding their skins, crabs shed their shells.

REPTILES, AMPHIBIANS, AND SEA CREATURES

The electric eel is the most shocking member of the eel family

The electric eel isn't a true eel. It's related to the carp family. This snakelike fish can kill a horse with the electric organs in its tail. It's a shocker to see, especially when it grows to be between six and nine feet long (1.83–2.74 m). No chance of meeting up with one, unless you are near a river or lake in South America.

Whales spout water

When whales come up to breathe air, they spout what appears to be a fountain of sea water. However, they are really spouting air, not water. Air that has been held in their lungs while they swim, heats up. When it hits the cooler air over the sea, it forms a steamy spray. The same sort of thing happens when you see your breath on a cold winter's day. The whale's spout is its breath as it exhales.

Each species of whale has its own way of spouting. Some spout straight up, some spout sideways, and others spout in a V-shape.

Horseshoe crabs are crabs

Horseshoe crabs are not crabs. A crab has a broad flat body covered with a shell. Its front legs have large claws, and it has five pairs of walking legs. A horseshoe crab has a large oval shell and a stiff, pointed tail. It has six pairs of walking legs and no claws.

Jellyfish are fish

They're not fish. They have no bones or fins. Jellyfish are practically all water, and a kind of jelly you wouldn't want to eat. Many are poisonous. Jellyfish belong to a group of animals called coelenterates.

Whalebone is whale bone

Articles made of whalebone aren't made of whales' bones. They are made of baleen, a material that hangs in fringed plates from the upper jaws of certain whales. The baleen strains minute organisms from the water, which the whales eat. Baleen is made of keratin, the same substance that makes up our fingernails. It is strong, but bends easily. In the past "whalebone" was used for the "ribs" of corsets and umbrellas. Today, plastic or metal are used instead.

Whales are the world's largest fish

Not so! Whales aren't fish. They are warm-blooded mammals. They cannot breathe underwater like most fish do. Whales have lungs and must return to the surface to breathe oxygen from the air.

REPTILES, AMPHIBIANS, AND SEA CREATURES

INSECTS

All insects are bugs	When the British talk about bugs, they usually mean bedbugs. Most of us use the term to mean any insect. Technically, the term bug applies to only certain types of insects with sucking mouthparts. Waterbugs, bedbugs, and plant lice are true bugs. However, ladybugs, mealybugs, doodlebugs, and sowbugs aren't bugs at all, even though you wish they would "bug off."
Flies can walk on ceilings because their feet have suction cups	If they had suction cups, they wouldn't be able to fly off as quickly as they do. Most flies have claws that enable them to cling to walls and ceilings. The common housefly has foot pads with hairs coated with a glue that enables it to have a safe foothold on glass and metal.
All insects eat and drink	Many kinds of adult insects don't eat. Mayflies, midges, and emperor moths are among the many living adult creatures that never eat. Adult mayflies may live only a few hours; adult emperor moths survive for about a week. Only the young of these insects eat and drink.
All mosquitoes bite	Only female mosquitoes bite. They need meals of blood to develop their eggs. The mouths of male mosquitoes are not able to pierce skin and suck blood. Males drink only water and plant juices.
Dragonflies sting	Dragonflies have been called "darning needles," "mule stingers," and "horse stingers."

INSECTS

According to folk belief, these fast-winged insects sew up people's ears and sting horses and mules to death.

However, dragonflies don't have stingers. They are completely harmless. That doesn't mean they wouldn't hurt a fly, because they dine on flies, mosquitoes, gnats, and many other small insects, which they capture and eat while flying.

Moths eat clothes

Any moth you see flitting about doesn't eat clothes. It couldn't even if it wanted to. Like all flying moths and butterflies, its mouth is a soft tube that can't bite into clothing.

It is the caterpillar of the clothes moth that dines on sweaters, coats, and blankets. But after spinning its cocoon, it stops eating and digesting wool forever.

Moths and butterflies grow

The tiny butterflies and moths you see flitting about will never grow bigger, and the ones with large wings and heavy bodies never were smaller. Caterpillars keep growing until they are ready to spin their magic boxes: chrysalises for butterflies; cocoons for moths. When the insects emerge with their newly grown wings, neither the wings nor the bodies grow. There are over 100,000 species of butterflies and moths, each with its own special size.

Certain beans jump

Seeing is believing: Mexican jumping beans jump. However, it isn't the bean that moves, but a tiny caterpillar living inside the bean. The caterpillar first eats the contents and then lines the inside of the bean with a web. It stops moving when ready to change into a moth, and hangs with its hind feet attached to the web. After growing wings, the moth comes out of the bean through a hole it made when it was a caterpillar.

Houseflies bite

Even if a housefly wanted to bite you, it couldn't. Houseflies have soft, fleshy mouthparts designed for sucking up liquids, not biting. If you're bitten by what appears to be a housefly, the culprit is probably a stable (horse) fly. Stable flies look like houseflies, but their mouthparts can pierce flesh. How unstabling!

Fireflies are flies

Dancing lights on summer evenings are caused by the well-known firefly. What isn't so well known is that fireflies are beetles, not flies. Beetles are easily distinguished from flies by their hardened front wings. They also have a second pair of wings that folds under the front pair, when not in use. Insects classified as flies have only one pair of wings.

All bees and wasps die after stinging

Honeybees die after their barbed stingers catch in the victim's skin and break off. However, many kinds of bees and wasps can sting more than once and not hurt themselves. Only female bees and wasps sting.

Bees take honey from flowers

The busy bees don't get honey from flowers. They get nectar, which they can eventually

INSECTS

turn into honey. Honeybees carry nectar back to their hives in special "honey stomachs." They spit out the nectar and place it in honeycombs, where it thickens and turns to honey.

Centipedes and millipedes are insects

These small, crawling creatures aren't insects. All insects have six legs. These creatures have many more.

Centipedes have one hundred legs

Although the name "centipede" means 100 legs, most centipedes have fewer than 50 legs. Some may, however, have more than 200.

Millipedes have one thousand legs

"Millipede" means a thousand legs. Most of these creatures have fewer than 200 legs to stand on. The young may have only six. More grow as they mature. The leggiest of all have 240 legs.

Worms are frequently found in apples

Several kinds of young insects are incorrectly called worms. The "worms" in apples are the larvae (young) of coddling moths or fruit flies.

Many insects go through different stages before reaching their adult form. For example, caterpillars turn into butterflies and moths. Inchworms and silkworms are also immature moths, and mealworms are beetle larva.

All worms are small

Most earthworms are less than ten inches (25.4 cm) long, but the giant Australian earthworm averages four feet (1.22 m) in length, and can grow to more than ten feet (3.05 m) long.

Earthworms come out of the ground to drink when it rains

On rainy days, earthworms come above ground, but not to drink. They come up out of the earth so they won't drown as the rain water goes into their ground holes.

Spiders are insects

They are arachnids, not insects. Their closest relatives are scorpions and ticks. A spider has eight legs, and its body is divided into two parts. An adult insect has six legs, and its body is divided into three parts.

All spiders weave webs

All spiders make silk, but some of these eight-legged creatures never weave webs. They use their silk to construct egg sacs and bind their prey, or they spin silk strands that enable them to float about. Wolf spiders run after their victims in order to devour them. Crab spiders lie in ambush waiting for prey to pass by. Jumping spiders pounce on their victims. They don't use silken snares.

INSECTS

Tarantulas are extremely dangerous

These large, hairy spiders (some with a leg span of more than ten inches (25.4 cm) look monstrous, but their bite is usually harmless to humans. Although some South American tarantulas can inflict serious bites, North American tarantula bites are rarely more serious than a bee sting. In fact, tarantulas are kept as pets by some people. They rarely bite, and are easy to keep.

Tarantulas don't spin webs. They catch insects by biting them with venom that turns the insects' insides into soup.

PLANTS

The peanut is a nut   It looks and tastes like a nut, but it's an underground member of the pea family.

A weed is a particular kind of plant   A weed is any plant that grows where it isn't wanted. Corn isn't a weed in a cornfield, but it is if it shows up in a soybean field. Dandelions, which are weeds to some, are lovely yellow flowers or delicious leafy green vegetables to others.

There are man-eating plants   Scary tales have been told about man-eating trees that grow in distant jungles. There are poisonous trees, but none that gobble you up. Trees have bark, but no bite.

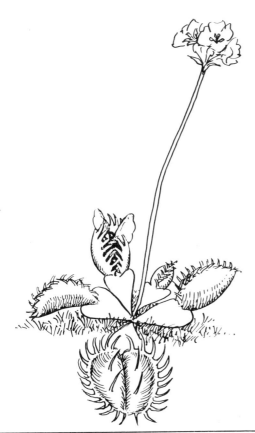

There are, however, plants that eat insects. The Venus flytrap has leaves that snap together like clamshells and imprison any insect that crawls on it. The pitcher plant has a leaf with a cuplike pouch. When an insect climbs into the pouch, a liquid inside enables the plant to digest the crawling creature.

PLANTS

Tulips originated in Holland

Centuries before the Dutch saw them, tulips grew in Mediterranean countries. The flowers were featured in Turkish gardens. Their bulbs were sent to Germany and Holland about the middle of the sixteenth century.

A craze for tulips, called "tulipomania," lasted from 1634 to 1636. Customers paid enormous sums for bulbs. One man paid approximately $5,200 for a single bulb. A dealer in Holland reportedly received a new carriage and two horses plus a large sum of money in exchange for one tulip bulb. Regular markets for tulip sales were established on the Amsterdam and Rotterdam Stock Exchanges. Rich people hoarded tulip bulbs as valuable investments. They didn't plant them in their gardens, but kept them locked in safes. When the price dropped in 1636, many lost their fortunes. The smart ones buried their investments and started the big business of cultivating Dutch tulips.

Healthy grass is green

Most of us think of grass as green because we associate grass with lawns and golf courses. However, there are thousands of kinds of grasses, and many of these aren't green. Wheat, oats, barley, rye, sugarcane, and bamboo are grasses.

Banana oil comes from bananas

Banana oil is a chemical compound that smells like bananas, but isn't made from bananas. The colorless oil is used in lacquers, glues, and heavy oilcloths. If you like the smell of banana oil, only put your nose to a banana fruit, not to the chemical. Should the fumes from the banana oil be inhaled for any length of time, your nose, lungs, liver, and kidneys could be damaged.

Forest fires harm all trees

Although they destroy, forest fires also help some trees to reseed. Intense heat opens the closed cones of some trees and releases the seeds of jackpine and lodgepole pine trees. The cones can hang for years without opening until a fire takes place.

Redwoods are the world's oldest trees

Compared with bristlecone pines, redwoods are young upstarts. The oldest redwoods are about 2,000 years old. The oldest known living tree is a bristlecone pine dubbed "Methuselah." It grows in California's White Mountains. As established by ring count, it is 4,600 years old.

All trees grow one type of leaf

Not true of the sassafras tree. It grows three different shapes of leaves, and all three can be found on the same branch. One leaf is oval, another mitten-shaped, and a third has three lobes with "thumbs" on each side. The mulberry tree also has three kinds of leaves.

Trees drink water from rainwater that falls on their leaves

Leaves are waterproof. They don't absorb rain. Trees receive their water from the ground, not from leaves.

PLANTS

Bamboos are trees

Although they can grow to be as high as a twelve-story building, bamboos are grasses, not trees. Like most grasses, bamboos grow in clumps. More than 200 kinds of bamboos grow in the tropical regions of America and Asia.

Orchids are rare flowers

There are more than 30,000 different kinds of orchids. All orchids have three petals, with the middle petal larger and differing in shape from the others. Although the biggest assortment grows in hot climates, orchids grow all over the world. They can be found in the Arctic Circle, in New England woodlands, and in mountains 10,000 feet (3.04 km) above sea level. Do you have a taste for orchids? The flavor vanilla is made from the seeds of several kinds of orchids.

White grapes are used to make white wine

Many white wines use red-skinned grapes. When the skin is removed, white wine can be made from either white, red, or black grapes.

Sugar maples are the only trees tapped for sap

Silver maples and red maples are also tapped for maple syrup. And the sap of date palm trees is used for sugar. In Mexico the sap of certain century plants is needed to make liquors called "pulque" and "mescal." Chicle from the sap of the sapodilla trees used to be the gum in commercial chewing gum until the 1940s, when it was replaced by synthetic gum.

Turpentine, waxes, paints, polishes, inks, and perfumes use saps from various kinds of trees. People all over the world tap sap for various purposes.

Water can easily be drawn from a barrel cactus

Many people believe that all you have to do to get water from a barrel cactus is punch a hole in it, and liquid flows. Not so easy! Although 90 percent of the total weight of the plant is water, extracting it is hard work. You have to chop off the top of the plant, scoop out the pulp, mash it with a stone, and then squeeze the stuff with your hands. Only then will a liquid be seen. Many people don't find the taste to their taste, but it does quench thirst. This "water barrel" plant has saved the lives of many desert travellers.

Indians used this cactus juice as a drink, and sometimes used the hollowed out trunk as a cooking pot. Today, cactus candies are made from the pulp.

Bananas grow on trees

There aren't any banana trees. Although they may grow to be thirty feet (9.14 m) high, banana plants aren't trees. They don't have solid stalks or trunks. Banana plants are herbs. An herb does not develop woody tissue, and dies down at the end of a growing season. The shoots of banana plants first bear flowers, then bananas, and then die. The next season new stalks grow from old roots.

Sponges are plants

Scientists thought that sponges were plants until about two hundred years ago. Now we know that all sponges are made up of multi-celled animals that cluster in colonies to make up the sponge framework. Until synthetic sponges were manufactured, people used sea sponges for bathing and cleaning. Over 4,500

PLANTS

kinds of sponges grow in oceans all over the world. Can you imagine one the size of a bathtub? There are sponges that big.

The first coffee plants were grown in Brazil

Farmers in Ethiopia and Arabia cultivated coffee more than a thousand years before America was put on the world map. At first, coffee was a food. The berries were dried, crushed, mixed with fat, and eaten. Coffee was also used to make wine. The skins of the berries were mixed with green beans and allowed to ferment. It wasn't until the thirteenth century that Arabs made a nonalcoholic coffee drink from the beans, or seeds, inside the berries.

In 1554, coffee was introduced to Europe by way of Turkey. In 1723, coffee plants were brought to America. They were first planted in Brazil in 1727.

Pineapples originated on the Hawaiian Islands

Pineapples weren't brought to Hawaii until the end of the eighteenth century. Columbus discovered pineapples in the West Indies. He brought samples of the strange fruit back to Europe. From there, sailors introduced the plants to Africa, India, and eventually Hawaii.

The century plant blooms every hundred years

Although the agave, or century plant, seems to take ages before it blooms, it never lives to be one hundred. Its name is misleading. Most century plants bloom and then die after eight to ten years; others live twenty to thirty years before blooming, and in some cases, they grow for fifty years before they bloom and die.

Plants can't grow under ice

Eelgrass grows in shallow water under ice. Eelgrass is a marine plant found on the Pacific coast.

Seaweed is a weed

It may be a weed to you if your feet become tangled in plants when you wade in the ocean, but it's not a weed to millions of people all over the world who use it as food.

Seaweeds are rich in vitamins and minerals. Many kinds make tasty soups, sauces, and other delicious dishes. Hawaiians have used seventy-five different kinds of seaweed in their cooking.

Seaweeds are also sources of important medicines. Some have been used to prevent scurvy, reduce fevers, and treat stomach disorders. For the past five thousand years, Chinese and Japanese have successfully treated goiters and other glandular troubles with seaweeds. Even today, marine plants are studied for the medicinal properties.

PLANTS

AMERICAN AND EUROPEAN HISTORY

Columbus discovered America

Columbus was not the first European to land in the New World. Almost five hundred years before Columbus, the Viking Eric the Red and his son Leif Ericson discovered Greenland. They or other Vikings may have discovered the coast of New England, also. British fishermen probably sighted parts of the North American coast during the 1400s before Columbus set out in 1492.

Columbus probably never knew about these northern voyages. They were of little importance, because they never resulted in permanent settlements. After Columbus's discoveries, on the other hand, there was rapid, widespread immigration and colonization of the New World.

The Declaration of Independence was signed July 4, 1776

As late as 1795, newspapers argued that the proper date of American independence was July 2. Although the Declaration was dated July 4, 1776, independence was actually declared two days earlier. On the fourth, John Hancock and Charles Thomson, the Secretary of Congress, signed the document, but many delegates refused. The official signing ceremony for most delegates took place on August 2.

Paul Revere made his famous midnight ride alone

On the night of April 18, 1775, Paul Revere, accompanied by William Dawes, rode to Lexington to tell people that the British were coming. At Lexington, Dr. Samuel Prescott joined them as they set out for Concord. Revere and Dawes were stopped by a British patrol. Prescott got through the British lines and completed the midnight ride. It was Prescott who alerted the Minutemen and enabled them to be ready to battle the British.

Revere became the famous hero because of Henry Wadsworth Longfellow's poem "Paul Revere's Ride." Longfellow neglected to give equal credit to Dawes and Prescott, who were also heroes of the famous night ride.

The American Revolution was a war against foreign troops

The American Revolution was mainly a civil war rather than a war against foreign troops. Washington, Franklin, Jefferson, and other American leaders had relatives who fought for the British king.

The number of those who revolted against England varied from colony to colony. New York State, for example, furnished more troops to the king than to Congress. Connecticut, Massachusetts, and Virginia, on the other hand, supported the Revolution.

Washington cut down a cherry tree

I cannot tell a lie. The story is legend, concocted by Parson Mason L. Weems in his biography of George Washington. The tale about the boy cutting down his father's cherry tree, and then confessing to the deed, was invented to prove Washington's honesty. The story proved a lot about Weems's honesty as a historian.

It was the custom of American Indians to massacre white settlers

There's more historical evidence that white pioneers massacred Indians. At least one thousand massacres against Indians have been recorded, beginning with one conducted by the Pilgrims in Connecticut. In 1637 they set fire to an Indian village. Five hundred natives were burned to death or shot while trying to escape.

There were, surely, Indian raids, but no massive massacres. When Columbus discovered America, there were approximately one million Indians in the area of the United States. By the end of the nineteenth century, there were only about one-quarter of a million Indians.

The Liberty Bell rang when the Declaration of Independence was signed

This legend was thought up by George Lippard, a Philadelphia journalist. In 1847 he wrote a sentimental story about a bellkeeper, "an old man with white hair and sunburnt face" and "a flaxen-haired boy with laughing eyes of summer blue" at his side. The old man supposedly rang the Liberty Bell while the small boy watched.

It's true that a bell did hang in the Philadelphia State House in 1776. John Adams reported that the bells of Christ Church chimed during the signing. But neither he nor anyone else mentioned hearing a Liberty Bell at the State House.

The bell wasn't given its name until the anti-slavery movement in the 1830s. The "liberty" referred to freedom for slaves, not independence for colonists.

AMERICAN AND EUROPEAN HISTORY

Betsy Ross made the first American flag

Some history books state that in 1776 Betsy Ross made the first flag, which she presented to George Washington, Robert Morris, and Colonel Ross, her husband's uncle. However, there is no record showing that these men received a flag from her. The story about Betsy Ross and the Stars and Stripes was not told until 1870—almost one hundred years later. And the tale was told by her proud grandson.

The American flag always had thirteen stripes

When Vermont and Kentucky joined the Union in the 1790s, Congress adopted a flag with fifteen stars and fifteen stripes. In 1818, Congress voted to change the number of stripes to thirteen.

The passengers on the Mayflower were Pilgrims

Of the 102 colonists, only 35 were Pilgrims, who lived in Leyden, Holland. The rest were called "Strangers" by the Pilgrims. They were poor people from England anxious to seek their fortunes in the New World. Eighteen of them had even agreed to work as servants for seven years, in order to pay for their passage. Eventually, the term "Pilgrim Fathers" was used for anyone who had come over on this ship.

Plymouth colony was the first settlement in New England

In 1607, thirteen years before the famous landing by the Pilgrims, a colony was established at the mouth of the Kennebec River in Maine. Unfortunately, the settlement was abandoned the following year, after the colony's leader, George Popham and many settlers died as a result of a harsh winter. The survivors sailed back to England. Plymouth Colony was the second settlement in New England.

The Pennsylvania Dutch came from Holland

The settlers weren't Dutch. They were German. English-speaking people probably confused the German word *Deutsch*, meaning "German," with "Dutch."

George Washington's birthday is February 22

According to his family Bible, "George Washington son to Augustine and Mary his wife was born ye 11th Day of February 1731/2 about 10 in the morning. . . ." The inscription isn't even sure about the year!

Lincoln's Emancipation Proclamation freed all the slaves

The Emancipation Proclamation freed slaves only in Confederate States and not in Kentucky, Maryland, and other slave-holding states that fought on the side of the North. It was issued in 1863, during the Civil War, which lasted from 1861 to 1865.

Lincoln deserves to be called The Great Emancipator not because of this proclamation, but because he urged Congress to adopt the Thirteenth Amendment, which abolished slavery in the United States. The Amendment was passed in 1865.

Pocohantas saved John Smith's life

The story about the Indian princess throwing herself on Captain John Smith to prevent him from being beaten to death is probably legend. Although the incident supposedly happened in

AMERICAN AND EUROPEAN HISTORY

1607, it wasn't mentioned in Smith's 1608 book, *A True Relation*. John Smith waited until 1624 to tell the tale of his rescue in his *General Historie of Virginia*. Smith was an expert at telling tall tales. For example, he wrote that he was once captured by Turks, sold as a slave, escaped, and then rescued a beautiful English woman who was also enslaved. Experts believe that Captain Smith had an overactive imagination.

America's first settlers lived in log cabins

Despite the many paintings showing Pilgrim Fathers returning to their log cabin homes, neither Pilgrims, Puritans, nor Virginia pioneers ever built log cabins. The first shelters

at Plymouth and Jamestown were similar to Indians' wigwams: saplings were bent U-shape like croquet wickets, then covered with turf, bark, or clay. Some settlers lived in hovels dug into riverbanks, roofed with poles and turf.

Swedish pioneers who settled in Delaware in 1638 were the first to build log cabins. Log cabins had been used in Norway and Sweden as far back as 800 A.D.

President George Washington lived in the White House

The White House wasn't built at the time Washington was president. George and Martha Washington lived in a small, three-story brick house in a poor section of New York City.

The White House was first occupied in 1800 by President John Adams. At that time, the building was unfinished and only six rooms were livable. First Lady Abigail Adams used the now famous East Room as a place to hang her laundry.

The term "White House" was officially adopted by President Theodore Roosevelt in 1902.

Scalping was an American Indian custom

Most people believe that all Indians took scalps, and that scalping was a primitive American practice. Although some American Indians collected the scalps of their enemies, many historians believe that they learned this grisly custom from Colonists.

White settlers paid bounties for dead Indians, and scalps were proof of the killings. By paying for scalps, Governor Kieft of New Netherlands cleared New York of Indians. In 1703 the colony of Massachusetts paid approximately $60 for each Indian scalp. In the eighteenth century, a male Indian scalp was worth about $134; a woman's was worth only $50. The practice of encouraging scalping by paying for disembodied hairpieces didn't stop until the middle of the last century.

The Pilgrims landed on Plymouth Rock

There's no proof that the story is true. Many historians believe that because of ocean currents, a ship never could have landed at the Rock.

The story about Plymouth Rock was first told by Thomas Faunce when he was 95 years old. He related it 120 years after the famous landing. Thomas told a crowd that his father, who came over on the Mayflower, pointed out the Rock as the place where the Pilgrims first landed.

New England Puritans burned witches

No one accused of witchcraft was ever burned at the stake in America. Fewer than fifty witch trials took place in New England. In Salem, witchhunt headquarters, nineteen were hanged, two died in prison, and one was pressed to death. The New England witchhunt was minor compared with the wholesale trials and burnings that took place overseas. Thousands of accused witches were burned at stakes in Europe.

All American witch trials took place in New England

Witch trials were held in many parts of the colonies. In 1685, Rebecca Fowler was accused and hanged as a witch in Maryland. In 1706, a Virginia woman was placed on trial and released. And in South Carolina, several people were punished for practicing witchcraft.

Mrs. O'Leary's cow started the Chicago fire

Mrs. O'Leary's cow never kicked the bucket that overturned a lantern that ignited a barn that burned a city. A reporter named Michael Ahern made up the story to add a flaming touch to his account of the Chicago fire.

Johnny Appleseed is a legendary character

There are many legends about Johnny Appleseed, but there are also true facts about this American pioneer named John Chapman, who lived from 1774 to 1845.

During the 1790s he worked his way west to the Pennsylvania-Ohio-Indiana frontier carrying a bag of apple seeds that he had collected from cider mills. Johnny planted trees and exchanged seeds for food and clothing. He was responsible for establishing numerous orchards, and deserves credit for spreading apple trees westward.

As a colorful, popular character in American history, he became the subject of many legends. For example, people claimed that because he loved every living thing, he put out campfires to keep mosquitoes from burning themselves in it. His adventures have been described in plays, poems, and storybooks.

AMERICAN AND EUROPEAN HISTORY

Johnny Appleseed Week is celebrated in Ohio the last week in September.

Mother Goose was a woman named Vergoose who lived in Boston

Despite the claims of Bostonians, there's no truth to the story. No one knows who wrote Mother Goose tales. Some say that Queen Goosefoot, also known as "Bertha with the Great Foot," was the original storyteller. Big-footed Bertha was the mother of the emperor Charlemagne.

In a volume published in America in 1760, credit for authorship was given to Nurse Lovechild, Jacky Nory, Tommy Thrum, "and other eminent authors."

Mother Goose exists in the minds of all children. She is that darling old lady with a high pointed hat and magic wand who travels on the back of a big goose, and spreads stories that delight all. But no one can prove who she was or when or where she lived.

Cleopatra was Egyptian

Seven Egyptian queens were named Cleopatra. None were Egyptian. They were Greek. The most famous Cleopatra, known for her love affairs with Julius Caesar and Mark Antony, probably didn't know the Egyptian language. She and the members of her court spoke Greek and dressed in Greek fashion. The royal city of Alexandria, (now Egyptian), was a Greek city at that time. Cleopatra was probably born in Alexandria.

John Cabot was English

His name was Giovanni Caboto, and he was an Italian, born in Italy in 1461. When Giovanni moved to England in the 1480s, he was known as John Cabot. Sponsored by England's King Henry VII, Cabot sailed in 1497 and explored the North American coast.

Hendrick Hudson was Dutch

The famous explorer was English. He worked for the Dutch East India Company. Although shipmates might have referred to him as Hendrick, the Dutch version of Henry, Henry never changed his name.

Nero fiddled while Rome burned

The Roman Emperor Nero lived during the first century. Violins weren't invented until the sixteenth century. At any rate, Nero wasn't even in Rome when a nine-day fire destroyed half the city. We will never know how the fire started. Nero blamed the Christians. This gave him an excuse to persecute them.

Joan of Arc was French

The famous heroine was not French. She was born in Domremy, part of an independent country called Bar. Bar didn't become part of France until 1776. Joan of Arc was burned as a witch in 1431. (She was not made a saint until the twentieth century.)

Medieval armor was so heavy that the wearer barely moved

Knights in armor didn't need derricks to hoist them into their saddles. They could move easily. The weight of a suit was about fifty pounds (22.68 kilos), which is not much heavier than some hikers' backpacks.

The bagpipe is a Scottish instrument

Bagpipes were featured in Roman coins that were used in Nero's time. The instrument has been played in North Africa, Arabia, France, Spain, Italy, Russia, and even in Scandinavia. King Henry VIII of England owned bagpipes. They have been as popular in Ireland as in Scotland.

Sir Walter Raleigh laid his cloak in mud for Queen Elizabeth

What a gallant gesture! Sir Walter supposedly put down his cloak and muddied it so that his queen wouldn't get her shoes dirty. The story was invented by Thomas Fuller years after Raleigh's death, and was repeated by Sir Walter Scott in the novel *Kenilworth*.

Raleigh didn't have to place his cloak in the mud to win the heart of his queen. She knighted him, granted him a wine monopoly, and presented him with vast land holdings in Ireland. As Captain of the Queen's Guard, he was near and dear to her.

Roman soldiers used chariots in battle

Assyrians and Egyptians used chariots in battle, not Romans. The Romans used chariots the way we use cars—for transportation. The Cadillac of the time was a chariot drawn by ten horses. The two-horsepower kind was used by commoners. Chariot racers used two, three, and four horses. On occasion, dogs and even ostriches were used. Chariot racing was such a popular sport in Rome that professional drivers sometimes raced twenty times in one day.

William Tell shot an arrow through an apple on his son's head

To tell the truth, William Tell never existed. Legends about men shooting apples from kids' heads are found in Swiss, English, and Norwegian folktales. It's all a lot of applesauce.

AMERICAN AND EUROPEAN HISTORY

The Gutenberg Bible was the first printed book

It is true that until the middle of the fifteenth century the only books available to Europeans were handwritten manuscripts. The first printed book of note was the Gutenberg Bible. However, the Chinese had discovered methods of printing at least a thousand years before. And in the eleventh century they used movable type for printing books. Europeans had to discover methods of printing independently, not knowing about the Orient's accomplishments.

Signing with an X was an indication that a person couldn't write

People usually assume that only persons who didn't know how to write signed documents with an X. However, before the seventeenth century, educated persons often used the X to sign official papers. The X, which symbolized the Sign of the Cross, meant that by their faith, the document was proper. Witnesses present to identify the "X-makers" often signed with signatures. The St. Andrew's Cross, which is like the letter X, the Cross of the Calvary, with a bar near the top, and the Greek Cross, resembling a plus sign, were all used on wills, deeds, royal decrees, and other important documents. Eventually the X was adopted by people who didn't know how to write.

The swastika is a Nazi symbol

Five thousand years before Hitler adopted it as a symbol for the Nazi party, the swastika was used in India as a good luck symbol. The word *swastika* comes from the Sanskrit *su* ("good") and *asti* ("to be"). The symbol was found on ancient coins in the Middle East. It also appeared in early Christian art, and in American Indian burial mounds.

Mummies are well preserved because of embalming

Although Egyptians had secret methods for embalming the dead, dry climate and the absence of bacteria were principal reasons for bodies' not decaying. Not only Egyptian mummies, but also bodies of animals that died in the desert thousands of years ago have been well preserved.

Magellan sailed around the world

In 1518 Magellan was in charge of a Spanish expedition that was expected to sail around the world. Magellan never completed the journey. He died before the voyage was completed. When ships landed at the Phillipines, natives killed him and some of his crew. One of his officers, Juan Sebastian del Cano, continued the expedition around the world. It arrived back in Spain in 1522.

Sir Walter Raleigh introduced tobacco to Europe

Sir Walter helped make smoking fashionable, but he wasn't the one who introduced the habit to Europe. In 1565 a naval hero, Sir John Hawkins, brought tobacco to England from Florida. Raleigh was about thirteen years old at the time—too young in his day to start that bad habit.

Raleigh is also falsely credited with having started the tobacco industry in Virginia. John Rolfe, who married Pocohantas, started the business of raising tobacco in Jamestown in 1612.

AMERICAN AND EUROPEAN HISTORY

Julius Caesar was a Roman emperor

In Caesar's time, Rome was a republic. The Roman Empire was founded seventeen years after Caesar was murdered. He was never crowned Emperor. His grandnephew Augustus became the first Roman Emperor.

The French Foreign Legion was stationed in the Sahara Desert

The Foreign Legion was assigned anywhere in the world where there was tough, unpleasant fighting. An assortment of thieves, cutthroats, and unemployed from various countries in Europe signed up—often with the misguided idea that life in the Foreign Legion held adventure and excitement. Life was usually harsh, exhausting, and boring. Although novels and movies have painted romantic pictures about them, legionnaires were often ordered to dig roads and ditches.

Only females were accused as witches

Although mostly women were accused of being witches, boys and men were also denounced. In some European communities male witches were more common than female witches.

INVENTIONS

Arabic numerals were invented by Arabs

We know that Arabic numbers originated in India because they were found in Hindu manuscripts that date back to the third century B.C. Arab traders and scholars learned the numbers and introduced them to Europe about one thousand years ago.

Galileo invented the telescope

Galileo was the first person to study the sky using a telescope. However, the Dutch scientist Hans Lippershey is usually credited as the inventor. Lippershey made a telescope in 1608, a year before Galileo built one for himself.

INVENTIONS

James Watt invented the steam engine

Watt never claimed that he invented the steam engine. During the first century A.D. Hero of Alexandria built elementary steam engines. Through steam power he had temple doors swing open, and he produced water fountains.

The first commercially successful steam engine was patented by Thomas Savery in 1698. It was used to pump water out of flooded mines in Cornwall. Thomas Newcomen patented a more efficient steam engine in 1712. James Watt used this engine for his own experiments. In 1769 Watt received a patent for an improved Newcomen engine.

Newton learned about gravity from a falling apple

Did a knock on the noggin make Sir Isaac think about the wonders of gravity? Myth has it that he was sitting under an apple tree when he was conked on the head by a falling apple. Newton was smart enough to think grave thoughts about gravity indoors, not in an orchard.

Edison invented the light bulb

Many scientists worked with incandescent lamps before Edison's time. In 1848 the English scientist Sir Joseph Swan experimented with light bulbs. But it was Edison who improved the light bulb and made it practical. He developed generators, motors, light sockets, safety conductors and many other devices for making electric lamps commercially successful. He organized companies to manufacture lighting equipment.

Robert Fulton invented the steamboat

Fulton deserves credit for improving steamboats and making them commercially successful. However, there were at least eighteen steamboat inventors before Fulton launched his *Clermont* in 1807. John Fitch was one. In 1791 he had a steamboat on the Delaware River that was scheduled to sail passengers between Philadelphia, Pennsylvania, and Trenton, New Jersey. It didn't attract customers, and his venture failed. John Stevens was another inventor who built a steamboat before Fulton. His craft, called *Little Julia*, sailed around New York Harbor in 1804.

INVENTIONS

Edison invented the phonograph to bring music to the masses

Thomas Edison believed that the main use for the phonograph would be "letter writing, and all kinds of dictation without the aid of a stenographer." He was surprised that his invention was used mainly for playing music.

Fingerprinting is a modern method of identification

Babylonian authors "signed" their writings by pressing their fingerprints on clay writing tablets. Fingerprints were also used as legal signatures on official documents in ancient China. Identification by fingerprint as we know it today was used about one hundred years ago in Britain. Fingerprint files identified government workers and prisoners in jails. During the late nineteenth century, the first large collection of fingerprint records was made by Sir Francis Galton. As a result of his work, Scotland Yard adopted fingerprinting in order to track down criminals.

Dr. Guillotin invented the guillotine

Dr. Joseph I. Guillotin was not the inventor of the head-chopper. He merely urged that the beheading machine be used to carry out death sentences in France during the French Revolution. Before it was used in France the device was used in Scotland, England, Germany, and Italy.

In France, the instrument of death was given the sweet name "Louisette" before it became known as a guillotine. In Scotland it was called "The Maiden." (Perhaps that's the origin of the idea that a man can lose his head because of a female.)

HEALTH

You can have growing pains	It may be emotionally painful to grow up, but it shouldn't hurt physically. So-called growing pains are usually the result of illness or muscle strain. If pains don't go away, call a doctor.
Exposure to cold causes head colds	The South Pole explorer Admiral Byrd couldn't catch cold when he was in the Antarctic because there were no germs there. A cold is an infection caused by a virus that is most frequently caught from others. It is not the result of a chill or a shiver.
A summer cold lasts longer than a winter cold	Colds do not last longer in summer. Watery eyes and stuffy noses that persist in summer may be caused by allergies, not by cold germs. Airborne pollen from plants can produce cold symptoms, therefore it may seem that "colds" during this season last a long time.
Eating pickles with ice cream will give you a bellyache	It's OK to have pickles with ice cream and herring with chocolate sauce. You won't bellyache unless the food contains unhealthy bacteria.
It is not healthy to drink water with meals	Water does *not* dilute the good qualities in food. In many cases, it actually aids digestion. Drinking during meals isn't harmful unless guzzling keeps you from chewing food properly. Saliva, stimulated by chewing, aids digestion too. Therefore, washing down food instead of using your "choppers" isn't smart.

HEALTH

Fasting is good for your health	A one-day fast won't hurt a young, healthy person, but prolonged lack of food can have serious effects on health.
Too much sugar causes diabetes	Diabetes is a disorder that prevents the body from using sugar. It has nothing to do with the amount of sweets one eats.
Diet pills cause you to lose weight	There is no pill or medicine that will cause you to lose weight and stay healthy. Too bad! If you want to slim down, eat less.
To cure frostbite, rub the frozen skin with snow	Believing this to be true, several Arctic explorers massaged their cheeks with snow when the temperature outside was 40°F (−40°C) below zero. Their faces froze. To treat frostbite, gradually warm the frostbitten area in warm water that is between 100°F (37.78°C) and 104°F (40°C). Then call the doctor.
Rabies come only from dogs	Cats, wolves, skunks, raccoons, groundhogs, squirrels, bats, and many other animals can carry rabies. By biting a person or another animal they inject the rabies virus. The disease is also spread if a person or animal touches the fresh wound of a rabid animal.
Anyone exposed to a slightly ill person merely risks becoming slightly ill	A person who isn't very sick can infect other people and make them very ill. You may have a mild case of chicken pox, but those who catch it from being near you may end up very ill.

Clean teeth prevent cavities	Not just cleanliness, but diet, general health, and heredity affect the condition of your teeth. Keeping teeth clean, however, can keep down the number of cavities by removing food particles that breed bacteria.
Whiskey cures snakebite	Instead of curing snakebite, whiskey can make the situation worse. Any alcoholic drink speeds the flow of venom through the body. If you want to use whiskey for snake bite, put the liquor on the wound in order to clean it. Then call a doctor fast! If you can't reach a doctor, apply a tight band above the wound, then cut and squeeze out the venom-filled area.
Hay fever is caused by hay and by goldenrod	A large variety of tree and grass pollens can cause an allergy termed "hay fever." Scientific tests have proven that ragweed pollen in the air, which can be seen under a microscope, is the most common cause of itchy eyes, runny noses and explosive sneezes. Ragweed plants grow in fields, near streams, and in vacant city lots. Goldenrod and hay are unfairly blamed, probably because the yellow flowers and haystacks are seen during the hay-fever season.
A fainting person falls backwards	Comedians who feign fainting fall back. People who lose consciousness and swoon in a faint fall forward or to the side.
It is unhealthy to keep flowers in a bedroom at night	Because flowers use oxygen and give off carbon dioxide, many people believe that a bouquet can spoil the air for the sleeper.

HEALTH

Actually, the amount of oxygen flowers use, and the quantity of carbon dioxide they give off, is very small and completely harmless. Just be sure to change the water in which cut flowers are standing so that they stay fresh and fragrant.

You can't get sunburned on a cloudy day

The sun's ultraviolet rays cause sunburn, and over 60 percent of these rays come through to you on a cloudy day. Rays reflected from water, sand, or snow can be strong enough to cause a nasty burn even on an overcast day.

Copper bracelets prevent attacks of arthritis

Copper jewelry has become big business because many people truly believe that the metal can keep their joints from aching. There's no scientific proof that copper is any more effective than wearing lockets containing crushed spiders—a practice common in some parts of the world.

Chewing hard foods strengthens the enamel on teeth

It strengthens your jaw muscles, but it doesn't affect the enamel—unless the food is so hard that it chips the tooth.

Heartburn comes from the heart

Heartburn should be called stomach burn, because the burning sensation you feel from indigestion has nothing to do with the heart. It comes from the stomach and esophagus, a muscular tube that leads to the stomach, and is usually the result of too much acid in the stomach.

Natural foods don't contain dangerous chemicals

Many foods contain dangerous chemicals. Cauliflower contains a thiocyanate that can hurt the thyroid gland. Lima beans have glycosides, which produce a cyanide poison. Coffee and tea have caffeine, a drug that can cause illnesses. Strawberries contain coumarin, which can prevent the blood from clotting. Carrots have carotoxin, a nerve poison.

You would have to eat about 400 carrots, one after another, before being poisoned. Foods don't poison you or harm you unless you eat an abnormal amount within a short time.

Pregnant women should not look at ugly objects because the experience might affect the baby

Some say that birthmarks are caused and shaped by some object an expectant mother sees. If a pregnant women is frightened by a mouse, there might be a mouselike mark on her baby. If she is scared by a snake, her child might have scaly skin. If the woman is horrified by an anteater—poor baby! All this is nonsense.

However, it's a good idea for an expectant mother to listen to beautiful music, go to museums, and read uplifting literature. She'll enjoy her pregnancy more, and the baby will have a more cultured parent.

Bacteria are harmful germs

Although some bacteria are harmful and cause a vast assortment of infections and diseases, many bacteria are useful and important for life. Bacteria in our intestinal tract help us digest food. Bacteria turn milk

HEALTH

into cheese, and grapes into wine. Dead plants and animals rot because of the action of bacteria. The rot enriches the soil, enabling plants to grow. Without bacteria, the world would turn into a desert, and life on earth would end.

Bacteria are single-celled organisms that can only been seen through a microscope.

FOOD AND DRINK

Heavy cream weighs more than light cream

Heavy cream actually weighs less than light cream! That's because heavy cream contains more fat, and fat weighs less than an equal amount of liquid. Heavy cream rises to the top if the milk is not homogenized. The term *heavy* refers to the thickness of heavy cream; not to its weight.

Cream weighs less than milk. It is composed of tiny drops of oil and fat that are lighter than the water and other parts that make up milk.

Chewing gum was first used in the United States

The ancient Greeks chewed gum made from the resin of the mastic tree. New England Indians were also gum chewers. Their gum was made from the resin of spruce trees. Chicle from the sap of the sapodilla tree used to be the gum in commerical chewing gum until the 1940s, when it was replaced by synthetic gum that is made in factories.

Soda is an American invention

Almost two centuries before the Pepsi generation was born, carbonated water was made by a British scientist. Joseph Priestley, called "the father of modern chemistry" is also "the father of soda pop." When he was experimenting with oxygen, an element he discovered, Priestley found out how to make carbonated water. Too bad this genius was never able to cash in on the billion-dollar soft-drink industry.

FOOD AND DRINK

Some companies have been able to bottle pure natural water	There's no such thing in nature as pure water. Minerals, gases, and other substances are always present. Some mineral content is desirable. Without it, the water you drink would taste "flat."
Buttermilk contains butter	The opposite is true. All butterfat is removed from milk in order to turn it into buttermilk.
Ketchup is a red-blooded American sauce	People of the Orient have been pouring ketchup into and on their foods for centuries. The words *ketchup* and *catsup* come from the Thai word, *kachiap*.
People avoid bitter foods that irritate the mouth	Black pepper, chili peppers, ginger, and alcohol are either extremely bitter or irritating to the sensitive parts of the mouth. Yet they are among the most sought after products in the world.
Marco Polo brought recipes for noodles and spaghetti from China	Someone dreamed up the myth that the famous Italian traveler brought the western world noodles, spaghetti and macaroni from China. The truth is that noodles are as old as wheat. Not only Chinese, but ancient Egyptians, Greeks, and Romans ate them. Before Marco Polo's time both Indians and Arabs enjoyed pasta dinners. The Indians called their dish *sevika*, and the Arabs called theirs *rishka*, both words meaning "thread." The Italian word *spaghetti* comes from *spago*, meaning "string."

Ice cream is an American dessert

Legend has it that Dolly Madison was the first person to serve ice cream. However, New England colonists enjoyed the dish long before Dolly was born. Ice cream was made in Europe for centuries. The Roman Emperor Nero featured the treat at royal feasts. His runners gathered snow in the mountains and jogged down to the royal kitchens, where chefs did a remarkable snow job. They added wines and fruits to make a cool dish fit for a king.

The best bananas are picked ripe

Bananas are picked green because they spoil if allowed to ripen on the plants. Those that turn yellow on the plant don't have the best flavor. The skin often breaks, and the fruit rots rather than ripens. Bananas are picked green because they ripen best off the plant.

Ice cream sodas cool you

They do, for a while. But the ice cream and syrup contain many calories. A calorie is a unit of heat. Calories warm the body.

Oxtail soup is made from ox tails

The stewed tails come from beef cattle, not from oxen.

Brown eggs have more food value than white eggs

Whether brown, white, or speckled, eggs have the same flavor and the same food value. Hens with brown earlobes produce brown eggs, and hens with white earlobes produce white eggs. Both hatch yellow chicks. There's nothing like a fresh egg, any hue, anyhow.

FOOD AND DRINK

While eating oysters you can hope to find a precious pearl

It's possible to find a shapeless, lusterless pearl in an oyster you eat. It isn't worth two cents. The common table oyster never has pearls of commercial value. Precious pearls come from types of tropical oysters that aren't very tasty.

The Earl of Sandwich invented sandwiches

John Montagu, fourth Earl of Sandwich, first Lord of the British Admiralty, earned a name in history as the inventor of the sandwich. The dish was named after him in 1762, the year he ate meat between bread as a time-saver when he gambled nonstop for twenty-four hours. He doesn't deserve the fame. Two thousand years before the earl's time, Romans were enjoying the dish. Sandwiches are probably as old as bread.

Hot meals are more nourishing than cold meals

Whether hot or cold, foods usually offer the same amount of nourishment. Hot foods can be *less* healthy if they are overcooked and vitamins are destroyed in the heating process.

Lemons are yellow when picked

Lemons are usually picked green. The fruit is then placed in curing rooms that have controlled temperature and moisture. Green lemons turn yellow in these rooms. When changing color they actually become tastier. Lemons are often kept in curing rooms for months.

Green oranges are unripe

There are ripe green oranges. Green ones are often riper than orange ones. When picked green, oranges are good to eat. These are often artificially colored before being shipped to market.

It is dangerous to eat oysters in the summer

It has been commonly believed that oysters "r" in season only during the months that contain the letter "r." In summer oysters are said to be poisonous.

When they come from clean, unpolluted beds, oysters are good to eat any time of the year. The original reason for not eating oysters in summer was old-fashioned, poor refrigeration, which caused oysters to spoil.

Eating like a bird means having a small appetite

On the contrary. Eating like a bird means having a whopping big appetite. Many birds can and do eat half their weight in worms and insects in one day. The American robin, for example, can gobble up seventy earthworms between sunrise and sunset.

Baby birds are miraculous eating machines. They digest food with uncanny speed. Their gaping mouths are continuously stuffed with caterpillars, beetles, and other insect delicacies. Some parents fly to their nests 20 times an hour in order to feed their hungry brood. Young titmice (not mice; they're birds) have been observed being fed 480 times in one day.

If you ate like a hummingbird, you would be devouring 285 pounds of meat every day.

According to the *Guinness Book of World*

FOOD AND DRINK

Records, the world's record meat-eater was a man who took forty-two days to eat one whole ox. That's not impressive, by any cuckoo's standards.

Soft-shelled crabs are a type of crab

The soft-shelled crabs you enjoy eating are hard-shelled most of their lives. A crab bursts out of its shell as it grows. It even sheds the armor on its limbs and the covering over its eyes. After a short time, it develops a new soft shell that eventually hardens and protects its body. The soft-shell stage is most sought after by people because of its rich flavor.

Pasteurizing kills all bacteria in milk

If all bacteria were killed off during pasteurization, you wouldn't be able to digest milk. There are bacteria that are bad for you, and bacteria that keep you healthy. Most of the "bad" bacteria have been removed from the milk you drink. But with every swallow, you get a mouthful of those microscopic, beneficial bacteria.

A sardine is a kind of fish

Small fish become sardines only *after* they are smoked, dried, or canned. Small fry of pilchards, herrings, and sprats are the most common fish fated to become sardines.

Jordan almonds come from Jordan

Jordan almonds have nothing to do with the river or country called Jordan. They come from Spain. The word *"Jordan"* originally was *jardin,* meaning "garden" in French.

Chop suey is a Chinese dish

You won't find it in the Orient—not even on Family Dinner menus. One food historian credits a Chinese cook with concocting the dish when he was working for the California miners, Forty-niners. Another writer believes that it started in a New York restaurant. Nobody ever claimed that chop suey came from China.

FOOD AND DRINK

YOUR MIND
AND
BODY

Your face reveals your character

Do you have wide, intelligent eyes? Are you thin-lipped and cruel? Does your jutting jaw show that you're a good fighter? Are you fat and jolly, or thin and sad? Do you have honest blue eyes, envious green ones, or flashing dashing black eyes that make you a hit with the opposite sex?

Any attempt to describe a person's character by analyzing appearance is pure folly. Whether criminal, saint, fearful, courageous, stingy, greedy, hot-tempered, cold, unfeeling—only actions, not appearances, betray you.

Here's an experiment frequently held in college psychology classes: the professor lines up pictures of criminals, and mixes them up with photos of clergymen and judges. Students are asked to determine which ones are criminals. Invariably, they fail to tell the difference between a thief and a chief of police.

Redheads have fiery tempers

Have you heard that redheads are hotheaded, blondes can't be trusted, and brunettes are sincere? Some folks claim that persons with fine hair are more sensitive than those with coarse hair. What superstition! There are fickle brunettes, faithful blondes, and mild-mannered redheads.

Palmistry is a science

Your future is not in the palm of your hand. There's no scientific evidence that your character, your past history, or your fate is etched in your palm.

YOUR MIND AND BODY

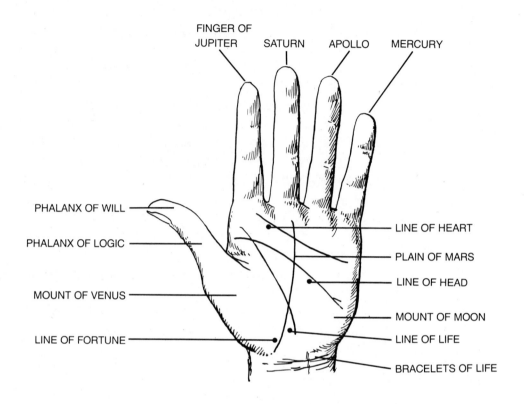

FINGER OF
JUPITER   SATURN   APOLLO   MERCURY

PHALANX OF WILL

PHALANX OF LOGIC

MOUNT OF VENUS

LINE OF FORTUNE

LINE OF HEART

PLAIN OF MARS

LINE OF HEAD

MOUNT OF MOON

LINE OF LIFE

BRACELETS OF LIFE

However, should you want someone to hold your hand and talk about *you* (your favorite subject), lend a hand to a palmist. You will learn about the love lump at the ball of your thumb, called The Mount of Venus. Your life line will be traced, and the Mount of Saturn at the base of your middle finger will reveal tales about your destiny. That's entertainment.

We have five senses

Ancient writers listed five senses: vision, hearing, touch, taste, and smell. Modern scientists have added additional senses: balance, pain, temperature, the senses of muscles, tendons, joints, and a visceral sense that gives us sensations about our internal organs.

Many people believe in a "sixth sense," which is often defined as the ability of one person to read another person's thoughts, or to foresee the future.

The duration of a dream can't be measured

Modern scientists are able to measure dream periods. They have found that although a person may believe a dream lasts a few seconds, it may last for more than half an hour. The longest scientifically measured dream lasted two hours and twenty-three minutes. You might be a record-breaking dreamer and not know it, because you haven't been tested in a laboratory.

There are people who never dream

Everyone dreams every night. By measuring eye movement, brain wave patterns, breathing and pulse rates, scientists have been able to find out just when a sleeper is dreaming. Most people dream about one-fifth of their sleeping time.

There seems to be a strong need to dream. Dreaming acts as a safety valve to release tensions, and it is a means of expressing wishes and fears.

Many persons are unable to recall dreams. However, scientists have found that an individual who never in his life remembered a dream will do so if awakened during that period of sleep when he is dreaming.

YOUR MIND AND BODY

The biggest brains belong to the smartest people	Differences in the weight and size of brains don't indicate differences in intelligence. An elephant's brain weighs about four times more than yours, and a whale's brain is about seven times bigger than your gray matter. Tall persons usually have heavier brains than short persons. Thus, they may have "higher" intelligence, but lower mental capacity.

A large brain can belong to an idiot, and a small brain to a genius. |
Acrobats are double-jointed	There's no such thing as a double joint. Some people have unusually flexible joints that enable them to bend their fingers, arms, legs, and backs in extraordinary ways.
Giants are strong	Giants in folk tales are monsters with super-human strength. In reality, giants (defined as persons over eight feet tall) are usually sluggish, sickly people. They move about crippled by the tug of gravity, which dooms their bodies sooner or later to break down. The life expectancy of a giant is less than normal. The condition of gigantism is caused by an overactive pituitary gland.
Drowning persons always come up three times	A drowning person can sink like lead immediately, or bob up and down any number of times.
Cutting hair speeds its growth	Cutting hair has no effect at all on its growth.

If you pull out one hair, ten will grow in its place	Balderdash! If this were so, balding men would be pulling out hairs in order to grow a thick top-crop. Only one strand of hair can grow from one hair bulb.
Hair can turn white overnight	A hairy experience can make you blanch with fear, but it won't change the color of your hair. The age at which you will become gray or white is inherited. It's in the genes.
Hair on men's bodies is a sign of strength	A man with hair on his chest may feel as strong as a hairy gorilla, but with the exception of Samson, who in the Biblical story lost his strength when his hair was cut, men don't derive power from hair.
Your body renews itself every seven years	The number seven has always been given mystical qualities: seven virtues, seven sins, seven years of bad luck, seven seas, seven graces, seven ages in the life of man. The ancient Greeks believed that our bodies are composed of seven substances. Like thirteen, seven is still a magical number. The body is constantly changing, but it's not renewed every seven years.
Oriental eyes are slanted	Even though they appear to be slanted, they are not. The effect is produced by a low nose bridge and a fold in the upper eyelid.

YOUR MIND AND BODY

Tears flow solely from the eyes

When you cry, your nose often gets runny. That's because some of the tears stay in the eyes and then go down a tiny tube that leads to the nose. Wipe your nose and dry your tears.

Your eyes are motionless when you stare

Even when you stare or glare, your eyes move. The muscles in your eyes move about 100,000 times a day, and never stop. Not even when you sleep. As a matter of fact, scientists test dream activity by measuring eye motion.

All taste buds are on the tongue

In addition to the 9,000 taste buds on your tongue, there are also taste buds on the roof of the mouth and at the back of the throat.

Butterflies and other insects have taste buds on the bottoms of their feet. They also taste sweet and sour through tiny hairs on their bodies.

Lemon juice removes freckles

Nothing can remove freckles, not even the most expensive beauty lotions. Most pigment cells that form freckles are below the surface of the skin. Lemon juice, like salve from ground-up beetles, is a folk remedy that doesn't work. Instead of trying to rub out those skin spots, relax, make lemonade, and remember that lots of people think that freckles are attractive.

Women have one rib more than men

Don't take a ribbing! Both men and women have twelve pairs of ribs. Even though Eve may have been made from one of Adam's ribs, males since the beginning of time have had the same number of ribs as females.

Both jaws move when you eat and speak

Try moving your upper jaw without moving your head. It can't be done. The upper jaw is fixed. However, you can hold your head still and move your lower jaw. (And you don't have to keep a stiff upper lip.)

The funny bone is a bone in your elbow

The funny bone is not a bone. It's a nerve that runs under the upper arm bone called the *humerus*. That's how it received its humorous name, even though there's nothing funny about the feeling you get when the funny-bone nerve is hit.

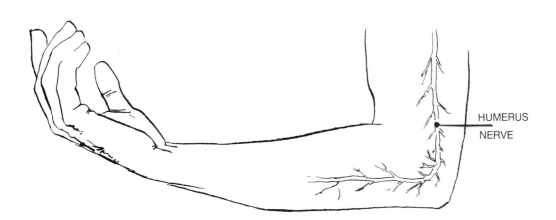

HUMERUS
NERVE

YOUR MIND AND BODY

Bones are the hardest substances in the body	The enamel that coats your teeth is harder than bone. However, unlike bone, enamel can't fix itself when damaged.
There are people who live to be more than 120 years old	Count St. Germain, a French nobleman who lived in the eighteenth century, claimed to be 2,000 years old—and many people believed him! His servant, refusing to reveal his own exact age, boasted that he had been working for the count for 500 years. Li Chung-yun of China reportedly died in 1933 at the age of 256. Despite these claims and those of yogurt eaters from southern Russia, there has never been proof that anybody has lived longer than 115 years. Those claiming to be older than 120 usually live in hard-to-reach parts of the world where no birth certificates are kept.
All your fingernails grow at the same rate	If you're right-handed, the nails on that hand will grow faster than those on your left hand. If you're a "southpaw," your left fingernails will grow faster.
It takes as much effort to smile as to frown	Seventeen muscles come into action when you smile. Forty-three muscles are needed for a frown. Save muscle power: Smile!

SPORTS

Abner Doubleday invented baseball

Strike out the story that Abner Doubleday created baseball at Cooperstown, New York, in 1839. You're off base! The truth is that Doubleday probably never played baseball, and that people in Cooperstown never knew about the game until after the Civil War.

The name and the game were known long before Doubleday's day. In 1744 *A Little Pretty Pocket-Book*, which was published in England, described "Base-Ball." The book was reprinted in America in New York City in 1762 and in Worcester, Massachusetts, in 1787.

Baseball's Hall of Fame was founded in 1939—100 years after the supposed creation of the sport there. What a publicity grand slam for a centennial celebration! It established Cooperstown as a prime tourist attraction for baseball fans.

Babe Ruth became famous as a hitter

He first became famous as a pitcher. Babe was a sensational pitcher for the Boston Red Sox from 1914 to 1919. His yearly pitching averages were fantastic. They ranged from .643 to .667. In 1916 he won 23 games and lost 12 and in 1917 he won 24 games and lost only 13.

Babe Ruth didn't become the famous "Sultan of Swat" until he was traded to the New York Yankees in 1920. During his career he hit 714 home runs.

Babe Ruth holds the home run record

Henry ("Hank") Aaron became the all-time home-run king after he hit his 715th home run as a major league baseball player. This

SPORTS

took place on April 8, 1974, when he swatted the ball over the fence while playing for the Atlanta Braves. This broke a record that had stood since 1935, when Babe Ruth hit his 714th homer.

Ping-Pong is a Chinese game

Ping-Pong is a trademark name for table tennis. It originated in the 1880s, when English army officers stationed in India thought up the game. They used a large table with a row of books across for a net, a champagne cork for a ball, and cigar-box covers for paddles.

Ping-Pong's singsong sound seems Chinese, but there's nothing Oriental about it. The Chinese, however, are well known for their excellence at the game.

Jujitsu originated in Japan

Jujitsu was developed by Chinese monks who devised trick holds to fight off bandits. The Japanese adopted the skill, and added grips that enabled fighters to kill opponents using their bare hands. For many centuries, the technique of jujitsu was kept secret and taught only to Japanese nobility.

Today this martial art is called judo. It's a sport that doesn't necessarily injure opponents (who know when to duck and when to twist an arm). Police and soldiers often disarm and injure enemies using judo.

Top spinning is child's play

Although children have always enjoyed spinning, the activity has also been a sport for adults. A Greek bowl that was made 2,500 years ago pictured two men spinning a big top by whipping it with sticks.

During the sixteenth century in Europe top spinning was an activity designed to keep people warm in winter. Lords of the land gave large whip tops to peasants. The strength and energy needed to whirl the top around kept them warm, or so busy that they had little time to think about the bitter cold weather.

Eskimo men have been seen with huge tops made of ice. One of them squats on top of the top, and others spin it. The rider enjoys a merry-go-round.

Adults in certain tribes of the South Pacific spin tops on their upturned feet, and on their big toes. Men from a Liberian tribe get tops spinning in the air by lashing them with whips.

In China and Japan, top spinning is a fine art that has been mastered by talented adult performers.

Checkers originated in Norway

Pharoahs were jumping opponents thousands of years ago. We know this because boards and checkers were discovered inside an Egyptian tomb. Before this discovery, the Norwegians were credited with playing the game during the eleventh century, then spreading it throughout Europe.

Football originated in England

The ancient Aztecs, Chinese, Greeks, and Romans played games in which a ball was kicked. A game called "futballe" was so popular in merry old England that King Henry II (1154–1189) became alarmed because he feared his soldiers would neglect practicing archery. He therefore threatened to imprison any players and anyone on whose land the game was played. The game was against the law in England for 400 years. It was made legal during the sixteenth century. By that time archery wasn't needed because firearms were used in warfare. King James I gave the sport his blessing, praising it as a clean, honorable, and manly pastime.

In 1863 many British football clubs formed an association and agreed to call the game association football. Americans call it soccer, a word that comes from the *soc* in association. In England and many other parts of the world soccer is called football. At least ten different forms of football are played in the world today.

Footballs are made of pigskins

Hogwash! Footballs were never made of pigskin; the leather comes from cowhides.

Badminton originated in England as an offshoot of tennis

The game's name certainly sounds very British, as does shuttlecock, that feathery object you hit over a net. Nevertheless, badminton is an ancient game that originated in India, where it was called poona. British army officers who played the game there in the nineteenth century brought it back to Great Britain. In 1873, the Duke of Beaufort featured it at a party given at his home in Badminton, England. That's how poona received its badminton name.

Chinese checkers is Chinese

The game is a modern version of an old English game. There's nothing Oriental about it.

Surfing started in Hawaii

When Captain Cook arrived in Hawaii in 1778 he was impressed with "the difficult and dangerous maneuvers which we saw performed" from surfboards. But even though Hawaiians had been surfing for centuries before Cook's tour, the sport probably originated in Tahiti, and came to Hawaii when the Tahitians migrated there more than 1,000 years ago.

SPORTS

Gut used for tennis rackets come from the intestines of cats

So-called catgut doesn't come from cats. It's usually made from the intestines of sheep or from nylon. Tennis rackets, stringed instruments, and threads used in surgery were often made of "catgut."

Ponies are used for polo

That's not the case anymore. Any horse fit to play the game can be mounted by a polo player. Many large horses are polo ponies.

Polo playing was always a sport

Would you believe that smacking a ball with a mallet while mounted on a horse was a religious ceremony? The riders hoped that by hitting a ball on the ground local gods would make crops grow. Polo ceremonies took place in Persia and Turkey.

The world's finest athletes competed in the Olympic Games of ancient Greece

Because the Olympics was a religious event dedicated to the worship of Zeus, no foreign athletes were allowed. All contestants had to be Greek citizens who had proved that they worshipped Greek gods. For many years women were not only barred as contestants, but they were forbidden to be in the audience. Any females seen near the games risked being put to death. Eventually, the ban against them was lifted.

After the Romans conquered Greece, in 146 B.C., athletes from many countries competed. A carnival spirit replaced the religious atmosphere of the Greek Games. Champions were awarded costly gifts and money, instead of the simple olive wreaths that crowned the champions of ancient Greece.

The yo-yo was invented by an American toy manufacturer

The ancient Greeks played with yo-yos. During the seventeenth century, French noblemen amused themselves with this throw-away-come-back toy. In the Orient, yo-yos have been used for hundreds of years.

The toy was brought to the United States from the Philippines in 1929. The term *yo-yo* means "come come" in the Philippine language of Tagalog. Therefore, that's the name of the game-game.

WEATHER

The North and South Poles are the coldest spots on earth

The Poles can be warmer than other parts of our planet. Temperatures at the North Pole are warmer on the average than those of Northern Siberia and Central Greenland.

The coldest permanently inhabited place is the Siberian village of Oymyakon, where the temperature reached minus 96°F (-71.1°C) in 1964. This village lies more than 200 miles (321.86 km) south of the Arctic Circle. The lowest temperature recorded was minus 126°F (-87.78°C) at Vostok, Antarctica, which is 900 miles (1,448.37 km) from the South Pole.

There is no snow in the tropics

You won't find any in the jungle, but if you climb a mountain you'll be able to enjoy a roll in the snow. The summits of Africa's Mount Kilimanjaro and Mount Kenya have snow, as do the peaks of South America's Andes and Mexico's Mount Ixtacihuatl. The feet of these mountains stand in the warm tropics, while their peaks are in a winter wonderland.

Sleet is freezing rain

Sleet and freezing rain are not the same. Sleet is made up of frozen rain pellets. Freezing rain is made up of liquid raindrops that turn to ice when they strike any object on the ground. Sleet does not stick to trees and wires. Freezing rain does.

A raindrop is pear shaped

Pictures taken with high-speed cameras show that a large raindrop is shaped like a doughnut with a hole not quite through it.

WEATHER

The eye of a hurricane is the center of a storm

Although it is often the center, the eye sometimes moves in various directions within a storm. The eye may be dry, and not shed a drop of rain. There may be no wind, the skies may be clear, and the sun or stars may be out. The eye is the calm area within a hurricane.

But the eye is a deceiver. Some people venture out into its calm believing that a storm is over. Then, quick as a wink, powerful winds and heavy rains start as the eye passes out of sight.

Lightning never strikes the same place twice

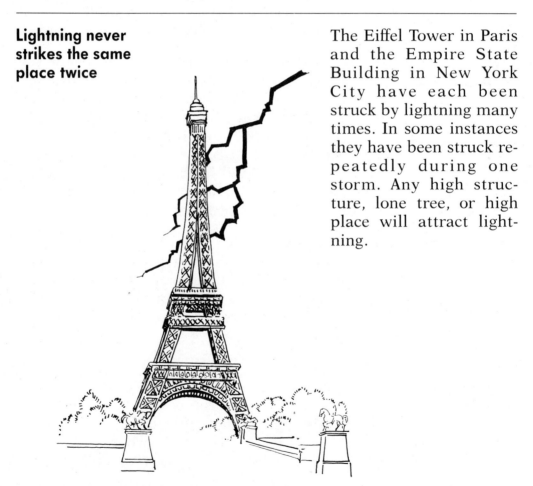

The Eiffel Tower in Paris and the Empire State Building in New York City have each been struck by lightning many times. In some instances they have been struck repeatedly during one storm. Any high structure, lone tree, or high place will attract lightning.

Fish can't rain down from the sky

Can you imagine a forecast: "Cloudy with periods of fish showers"? It has rained fish. Waterspouts have lifted fish high in the air, and strong winds have landed them inland. In 1817, a downpour of herrings came down at Appin, Scotland.

Hurricanes and tornadoes lift all sorts of creatures up, and often carry them hundreds of miles. In 1900, after a violent storm, frogs and assorted insects rained down in parts of England. However, despite all the talk, it has never rained cats and dogs.

Hailstorms can't kill people

Hailstones as large as oranges came down during a violent storm in India, in 1888. Hail is made up of rounded pieces of ice that fall to earth, usually during thunderstorms. More than 200 people were killed, and over 1500 cattle, sheep, and goats died as a result of that Indian hailstorm. A hailstorm that took place in China in 1932 killed 200 people and injured thousands. It also destroyed houses, crops, and animals in 400 villages.

The largest hailstone found in the United States was five and a half inches in diameter.

Sometimes people have been knocked unconscious and buried under several feet of hailstones. Then they die of cold and exposure.

Large hailstones cause more damage than small hailstones

Hailstones the size of baseballs don't cause as much damage as those the size of marbles, because fewer of them fall.

WEATHER

A drought means there's no rain

It may rain, but a drought takes place when there is not enough water to meet the needs of animals and plants. Farmers might call the scarcity of rain a drought, while city dwellers might not. A drought in Cairo, Egypt, which normally has 1.1 inches of annual rain, is different from a drought in New Orleans, Louisiana, where 64 inches of rain is expected each year.

Floods are always unfortunate

In most cases, a flood is a catastrophe. However, in some instances it is a blessing. In Iraq, parts of China, Cambodia, and Egypt, floods are considered a blessing. When rivers overflow they enrich the soil of the surrounding land, and make agriculture possible. The rising of the Nile River, for example, has been a source for celebration for thousands of years. Crops thrive along its banks. One can easily detect where the flood waters end, because that's where barren desert begins.

Sandstorms have buried people alive

This takes place in the movies and in fantastic tales of adventure, but not in real life. Sand does not pile up on the ground the way snow does. Even in sandy deserts, it may take years for a dead animal to be covered by sand.

Sandstorms are dangerous, even though they don't bury people alive. They cause people to lose their way and die of thirst.

Floods don't take place in deserts

Violent storms sometimes take place in parts of the desert where rain hardly ever falls. The flooding rains often rip out roads, and turn sand valleys into ponds. But the water usually disappears quickly. It sinks down underground, or it is evaporated by the hot, dry desert air.

WEATHER

LAND,
SEA,
AND SKY

Earthquakes rarely take place

There's an earthquake somewhere on our planet every minute! Fortunately, only ten to twenty quakes per year are strong enough to do damage, and most of these take place under the ocean or in remote regions where few people live.

In some countries, such as Japan, earthquakes occur almost every day, but most of these are tremors that cause no damage. One that took place in 1923 in Tokyo and Yokahama killed more than 100,000 and wrecked both cities. In 1976, an earthquake in China was responsible for the deaths of 655,000 people.

The most famous earthquake in North America took place in 1906 in San Francisco, California. The tremors caused fires that resulted in the deaths of about 700 persons.

A small earthquake prevents a large one

Wishful thinking for those who quake at the thought of a catastrophe! A small earthquake does not act as a safety valve that relieves underground pressure. There may be a series of small quakes, or a huge earthquake, before or after a minor shake-up.

The earth is always cool beneath the surface

Anyone who has ever toured an underground cavern knows that this is a cool experience. But if you conclude that the farther down you go, the colder it gets, you are wrong. The lower down you go, the hotter it gets. Although the center of the earth has never been measured, scientists estimate that the heart of our planet is between 4,000°F (2,204.44°C) and 7,500°F

LAND, SEA, AND SKY

(4,148.89°C). That's hotter than Hades was ever supposed to be.

All volcanoes are on land

The ocean floor has at least 10,000 volcanoes. Sometimes when a volcano erupts, lava flow builds up, juts out of the waves, and creates a new island. Many scientists were able to watch and photograph the development of a new island created by an undersea volcano. They watched the island of Surtsey, which was born in water just south of Iceland on November 5, 1963. A Caribbean volcano called Kick 'em Jenny is expected to grow up under water and become an island before the year 2000.

Mt. Everest is the world's highest mountain

Kauna Kea Mountain in the Hawaiian Islands is 756 feet (230.43 m) taller than Mt. Everest. It is 13,784 feet (4.2 km) above sea level plus 16,000 feet under water. That totals 29,784 (9.1 km) feet. Mt. Everest is 29,028 feet tall (8.8 km).

The Himalaya mountain range is the largest on earth

The largest range can be found snaking through every ocean on earth. It is the Mid-Oceanic Ridge, and it winds itself around our planet like the seams of a baseball. Greater than the Himalayas, Rockies, and Andes combined, it covers as much of the earth as all continents combined. Most of the peaks are more than a mile below the waves. Some are over 20,000 feet (6.1 km) high.

Deserts are mostly sand

Most of us picture deserts as sand dunes that stretch as far as the eye can see. In reality deserts have mountains, canyons, rocks, cliffs, and even lakes and pools. Of the Sahara's three and a half million square miles (9.07 million square km) only one-tenth is sand. The rest is composed of rocky hills, mountain ranges, gravel beds, dry river beds, and oases with water and green vegetation.

About one-fifth of the world's land surface is classified as desert. A desert is an area that receives less than ten inches of rainfall a year.

There's no such thing as singing sand

Sand not only sings, but it whistles, squeaks, and booms. It whistles and squeaks when someone walks on it, or jam a stick into it. It booms whenever there's a sand avalanche.

Mirages are the result of overactive imaginations

A throat-parched man lost in a desert, delirious, near death, suddenly sees a lake. With his last burst of energy, he rushes toward it, only to discover that the lake doesn't exist. He has seen a mirage.

But the mirage was not necessarily a sight he dreamed up. Mirages actually take place under certain weather conditions. They can even be photographed. Pools of water that don't exist can be seen not only in a hot desert, but over hot pavements. Most of us have seen mirages on highways. They look like wet puddles until you drive close to them.

Mirages are often reflections of real things. A blue sky reflected on the ground can look like water. At sea, a mirage can be an upside-down image of a ship floating in air, or a faraway boat that seems close by. On land, it can be an upside-down city reflected in the sky, or a river that seems to flow through the clouds. Images of everything we see are formed by light rays that bounce and bend when they travel between cold and warm air. When light rays from rivers and buildings bend upward, their images hit the sky.

Quicklime destroys dead bodies

Murderously untrue, despite the number of who-done-its that feature quicklime destroying corpses. Quite the opposite is fact: quicklime can preserve a body and prevent it from decaying. Belle Gunness of La Porte, Indiana, was convicted after fourteen of her victims were found preserved in quicklime.

Glaciers move so slowly that their advance is hardly noticeable

Many glaciers move less than half an inch (1.27 cm) a day. However, there are many that advance more than 65 feet (19.81 m) each day. The Black Rapids Glacier in Alaska advanced a daily average of 115 feet (35.05 m) during the winter of 1936–37.

Until Columbus's time people believed that the earth was flat

Columbus wasn't the first to believe that the earth is round. Most educated people of his time knew that our world wasn't as flat as a pancake. In fact, for at least one thousand years before Columbus, scholars assumed that the world was a sphere. During the second century A.D. the famous astronomer Ptolemy proved it by noting that during an eclipse the earth's shadow on the moon was round.

Animals can always receive sufficient drinking water from snow

Believe it or not, wild animals and livestock have died in blizzards because they lacked water, not because of the cold. Body heat can usually keep an animal alive in an icy storm, but some creatures, such as cattle, can't lick enough snow for their water needs. During a blizzard, farmers have to provide water for their animals.

The Arctic is a frozen wasteland

There are remote regions where there is perpetual ice and snow, but the Arctic is not an all-white wilderness. Some parts have crops that grow during the summer months of continuous sunlight.

Two hundred miles (321.8 km) north of the Arctic Circle people grow hay, wheat, and a variety of vegetables. Cabbages weighing thirty pounds are common.

Summer heat of 85°F to 90°F (29.4°C–32.2°C) takes place in many parts of the Arctic.

A bog is a swamp

Here's the difference: A swamp has trees. A bog may contain plants and grasses, but not trees. A *marsh* is like a bog. A *morass* has trees, and is, therefore, a swamp. Don't get bogged down by words. Each has a special meaning.

Underground water is hard to find

If you dig deep enough, the chances are you'll find water almost any place on earth, even under deserts. The problem is that in many places water lies so deep that it costs too much to drill and pump it up. Also, water is often too polluted to be used.

LAND, SEA, AND SKY

Water dowsing works

There are people who claim that a Y-shaped forked stick from a birch or ash tree is a perfect "divining rod" for finding underground water. The person with the stick is called a dowser, and the process is known as water witching.

The dowser's technique is as follows: One fork of a stick is held in each hand. The palms of the hand are held upward and the end of the stick is held up. When the end points down, it means that water is present in the ground.

Dowsers claim that the forked stick points down without being moved by them. However, tests prove that the dowser's muscles

move, and that forked sticks often point to dry spots. Scientists investigating the effectiveness of water witching have not found a forked stick that works. Nevertheless, there are about 25,000 professional dowsers in the United States.

If you could dig through the earth you would land in China

The antipode, or opposite side, of the earth from the United States is part of the Indian Ocean between Australia and South Africa. Can you dig that?

Spring tides take place in the spring

Spring tides take place at any season of the year, during full moon and new moon. In this case, the word *spring* means "jump." It doesn't refer to the season.

Tides cause tidal waves

Tides have nothing to do with it. Large, destructive ocean waves, mistakenly known as tidal waves, are caused by earthquakes, coastal landslides, or volcanic eruptions. The technical names for giant sea waves of this kind are "tsunami," or "seismic waves."

When the Indonesian volcano Krakatoa erupted in 1883, it created a wave that reached a height of 120 feet (36.58 m); 36,000 people were killed. Traveling at speeds of 350 to 450 miles per hour (563.26–724.19 kmph), the wave's passage was traced as far as Panama in Central America.

The most destructive tsunami took place in 1703 at Awa, Japan. It killed more than 100,000 people.

LAND, SEA, AND SKY

Icebergs can be found only in polar waters

Swift currents have carried icebergs into warmer waters. An average of four hundred icebergs drift south of Newfoundland each year. Some have been found as far south as Bermuda and the Azores.

The largest icebergs, however, are found in the Antarctic. In 1956 a Navy icebreaker reported one that was 208 miles (334.73 km) long and 60 miles (96.54 km) wide. The largest northern iceberg was sighted in Baffin Bay in 1882. It was seven miles (11.27 km) long and three and a half miles (5.63 km) wide.

After the *Titanic* struck a huge iceberg south of Newfoundland in 1912, an International Ice Patrol was formed. Since that time, no life has been lost because of an iceberg collision.

Icebergs are made of frozen sea water

Icebergs are made up of fresh water. They are chunks of glaciers that move down from polar regions and break off into the sea. (Glaciers are large masses of ice and snow that form in areas where the rate of snowfall exceeds the rate at which the snow melts.) Icebergs can be thousands of feet high and many miles wide. The largest part of an iceberg is below the water. Only 1/9 of it appears above the surface.

Because many parts of the world suffer from water shortages, plans have been proposed to hitch tugs to icebergs and haul them to distant lands. The Iceberg Transportation Company, a Saudi Arabian firm formed in 1977, has a $100 million project:

pulling a 200-million-pound (90,720,000 kg) iceberg 6,000 miles (9,655.8 km) from Antarctica to Saudi Arabia. That's like bringing a mountain to Mohammed!

Ocean water never freezes

If it gets cold enough, ocean water will freeze. *Sea ice* is frozen salt water. In winter chunks of sea ice cover about 5 percent of the northern oceans and 8 percent of the southern oceans.

The ocean floor is flat

The deep sea has mountains higher than Mt. Everest, and ranges bigger than all the mountain ranges on land. There are hills, valleys, ridges, plateaus, as well as flat plains at the bottom of the sea.

Ships have been trapped in Sargasso seaweed

The Sargasso Sea is a sea within the ocean that stretches more than halfway across the Atlantic. Millions of tons of weeds float in its waters.

Sailors used to believe that the weed masses stopped ships and trapped them forever. There were stories of skeletons on rotting hulks that were entangled in masses of vegetation. These tales don't hold water! The sargassum weeds aren't strong enough to trap a rowboat. Although they form clumps, the plants are widely scattered over 50,000 square miles (129,500 sq. km).

LAND, SEA, AND SKY

Undertows are dangerous to swimmers

The undertow myth has been undermined by scientists at Scripps Institution of Oceanography. They found that although there can be a slight undertow, dangerous currents that cause drownings move out to sea at the surface of the water.

Sound can't travel far in water

What an unsound notion! Water is a better conductor of sound than air. And in water sound travels almost five times faster than in air. In air the explosion of a one-pound block of dynamite can be heard for half a mile (.8 km). That same explosion would travel thousands of miles in the ocean.

In 1960, scientists from Columbia University set off depth charges off the coast of Australia. The sound reached Bermuda, almost halfway around the world, two hours and twenty-four minutes later.

The sea is silent

The ocean can be as noisy as a tropical jungle. Fish croak, grunt, whistle, honk, and squeak even though they have no vocal cords. They make these noises by grating teeth that grow deep in their throat, by rubbing fins against their sides, or by drumming inside muscles against their air bladders. Some snap their fins or gnash their teeth.

Humpback whale songs are among the loudest sounds. These remarkable creatures compose melodies that can last half an hour. Sometimes the high voices of young males join in chorus with the adult basso voices. Recordings of their songs are big sellers, especially among those who like modern electronic music. In addition to wails, chirps, snores, and hums, there are noises that sound like airplanes taking off, cars jamming on brakes, and giants having hiccups.

Some objects drift forever in ocean waters

Everything that enters the ocean sinks to the bottom, even a feather and a speck of dust. People used to believe that sunken ships drifted in mid-waters. We now know that the floor of the sea is the destination for everything that sinks. Not only sunken ships, but skeletons (mainly of sea creatures), soft drink bottles, and other trash thrown overboard litter the bottom of the ocean. Eventually, even bottles with messages inside sink.

On a clear night, you are able to see millions of stars

Although there are as many stars in the universe as there are grains of sand on all the world's beaches, you can't see more than 4,000 stars with the naked eye. Of the stars that can be seen from any one place on earth, only half are visible at one time, because the others are below the horizon.

If you started counting the stars you could see on a clear night, you probably wouldn't be able to count more than 1,000. However, through the powerful telescope at Palomar Observatory in California, scientists can photograph more than one billion stars.

LAND, SEA, AND SKY

If you put your ear to a seashell you will hear the roar of the sea

When you hold a spiral seashell to your ear, you do hear noise. You are listening to ordinary sounds echoing as air inside the shell vibrates. The sound of blood rushing through your ear may be amplified, so that your ear may also be listening to your own ear.

Stars don't have color

There are red, orange, yellow, white, blue, violet, and green stars. Stars come in every color. Their hues can be seen when you examine them through a telescope.

Colors tell the scientist the temperature and the elements that make up the stars. Usually the blue and white stars are the hottest, and the red ones are the coolest. The sun is a yellow star that is medium hot.

A nova is a new star

A nova is not a new star. It is an existing star that explodes and becomes very bright.

About twenty novas are observed each year. They blaze into view, then slowly fade to their former faintness. There are many novas that are never noticed because even at their brightest they are too faint to be seen.

One of the most brilliant novas was discovered by the astronomer Tycho Brahe in 1572. It was so bright that it could be seen during the day. Tycho's nova gradually lost its brightness, and after sixteen months it could no longer be seen.

Scientists still can't explain why certain stars explode. Heaven knows!

Stars look large when viewed through a telescope

They look brighter, not larger. Stars are so far away that all one ever sees is the light coming from them. Light can't be made larger, but it can be made brighter.

The telescope enables you to see more stars because it collects light from stars too dim to be seen by the naked eye.

Shooting stars are stars

Shooting stars aren't stars. They are meteors. A meteor is a streak of light seen in the sky when a chunk of matter from outer space enters the earth's atmosphere and burns up. A star is a mass of glowing gas. The sun is a star.

Fixed stars are motionless

All stars travel rapidly through space. The term *fixed star* refers to those that *seem* to keep the same distance from other stars in the sky.

LAND, SEA, AND SKY

The sky is blue

The hue is blue to you because of dust particles and droplets of water in the air. But above the atmosphere the sky is black. Astronauts have seen the jet black of the sky unpolluted by our atmosphere.

The sun does not affect tides

The moon is famous for its pull on earth's waters. But the sun affects tides also. However, because the moon is closer to earth, it has twice the effect.

The sun is about the same size as the moon

The sun is about 400 times the diameter of the moon. It's also about 400 times as far away from earth as the moon. Sun and full moon just seem to be the same size. But, any round objects—a dime, a ball, or a pizza—if held far enough away from the eye can appear to be the same size as the sun or full moon.

The sun stays still as earth revolves around it

The sun is a star and, like all stars, it travels rapidly through space, while earth circles it at the rate of 66,500 miles (107,018 km) per hour. The sun's pull (gravity) holds the earth in an orbit around it.

The sun is closer to earth in summer

The sun is closer to earth in winter than in any other season. It's about 3 million miles (4,827,900 km) closer to our planet than in the middle of the summer. However, the earth is tilted toward the sun in summer and away from it in winter. Therefore, the sun strikes us more directly in July and August. Get the angle?

There are seas and oceans on the moon

If you look at a map of the moon, you will see the names of seas, oceans, bays, marshes, lakes, and lagoons. Astronomers used to believe that the dark areas of the moon were covered with water, and therefore gave them names like Sea of Moisture, Lake of Dreams, Marsh of Sleep. Neil Armstrong landed in the middle of the Sea of Tranquility. Astronaut Alan Bean explored the moon's Ocean of Storms. Neither of them could get his feet wet. The moon is dryer than dust. There's not a drop of water on the lunar surface.

The first serious space travel proposals were made after World War II

As early as 1891 a German inventor, Hermann Ganswindt, lectured about space travel, and predicted that it would take place during the twentieth century. A Russian scientist, Konstantin Ziolkowski, actually designed a spacecraft with rockets in 1903. His ideas sounded unsound and therefore weren't taken seriously.

Rockets were invented during the twentieth century

The Chinese used exploding rockets 750 years ago during a battle against Mogul invaders. Shortly thereafter, rockets were adopted by armies in Europe and the Middle East. By the sixteenth century, rockets were no longer important in land warfare because guns became the big shots. However, at sea, ships were targets for rockets. The "rockets' red glare" was seen when the British attacked Fort McHenry during the War of 1812.

LAND, SEA, AND SKY

The first UFOs were reported during the twentieth century

Down through history strange objects and unusual glowing lights in the sky were reported by people all over the world. Thousands of years ago, giant saucers were seen flying over Japan, China, and Egypt. During the Middle Ages, seeing UFOs became common. Unidentified Flying Objects inspired the Emperor Charlemagne to declare that anyone who landed from the sky was a criminal subject to arrest. Every era in history had its UFO sightings. During the 1890s in America, thousands of people reported blobs, ships, saucers, and mysterious circles in the sky.

The modern age of UFOs started in full force in 1947, after an airplane pilot reported a flying saucer. Ever since then, governments and private UFO clubs have kept written records of UFO reports.

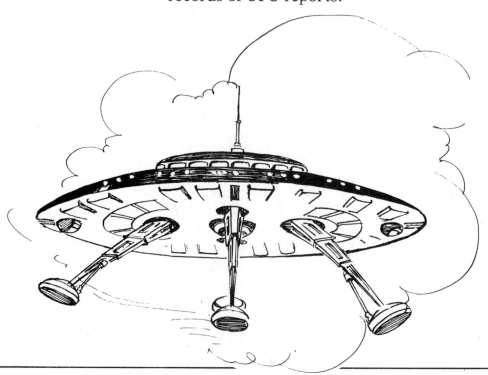

INDEX

Adams, John, 71,75
Aging, human, 115, 118
Allergies, 93, 95
America: colonization of, 71, 72, 73–
74, 76; discovery of, 69, 79 *See*
American Revolution, Flags,
Indians.
American Revolution, 69–70, 71–72
See Adams, Washington.
Animals: babies, 14–15; largest,
37,47; that "play dead," 17–18, 41;
tool-making, 11–12; water-drink-
ing, 14, 143; weather forecasting
by, 22, 24, 32, 33 *See* Birds, Mam-
mals, Marsupials, Rodents, Snakes;
See also name of animal.
Antarctic, 131, 146–147 *See* South
Pole.
Antlers, 14
Appetite, human, 105–106
Appleseed, Johnny, 77–78
Arctic, 94, 143,146 *See* North Pole.
Armor, medieval, 80
Arthritis, 96

Babies, size of, 14–15
Bacteria, 95, 97–98, 106
Badminton, 125
Bagpipes, 80
Bald eagles, 32
Baldness, 115
Bamboo, 62
Banana oil, 60

Bananas, 60, 63, 103
Baseball, 121; records, 121–122
Bats, 15–16, 94; vampire, 16
Bears, 18, 24–25; North American
Black, 14–15, 25
Beavers, 14
Bees, 26, 53–54
Bible, Gutenberg, 82
Birds, 29–34; appetite of, 105–106;
egg-laying, 29, 31; flying, 30, 32, 34;
nest-building, 29; sleeping habits
of, 29; tool-making, 11 *See* name of
bird.
Birth defects, 33
Birthmarks, 97
Blackbirds, 34
Boa constrictors, 40
Body, human, 111, 114, 115–118 *See*
Human beings.
Bogs, 143
Bones, human, 117-118 *See* Fossils.
Bugs, 51 *See* Insects.
Bulls, 21, 45
Butterflies, 52 *See* Caterpillars.
Buttermilk, 102

Cabot, John, 79
Cactus, barrel, 63
Caesar, Julius, 78, 84 *See* Rome.
Camels, 16
Canary birds, 34
Canary Islands, 34
Capybara, 20 *See* Rodents.

Caterpillars, 52, 54
Cats, 19, 94, 126
Cavities, 95, 96
Centipedes, 54
Century plant, 64
Chameleons, 42
Chariots, 81
Checkers, 124; Chinese, 125
Chicago fire, 77
Chickens, 31, 103
Chimpanzees, 11–12
Civil War, American, 73
Cleopatra, 78 *See* Egypt.
Coffee, 64, 97
Color blindness, animal, 21
Columbus, 69, 71, 142
Common cold, 93
Cosmetics, 116
Crabs, 45, 106; Horseshoe, 46
Cream, 101
Crime, 90, 142
Crocodiles, 42
Crows, 32

Declaration of Independence, 69, 71
Deserts, 134–135, 141
Diabetes, 94
Dieting, 94
Dinosaurs, 37–38
Dodos, 30
Dogs, 20, 24, 94
Doubleday, Abner, 121
Double-jointedness, 114
Dowsing, water, 144
Dragonflies, 51–52
Dreams, 113
Droughts, 134
Drowning, 114

Earth, 152; center of, 139–140;
    fallacies about, 142, 145
Earthquakes, 139, 145
Eating: human, 93, 94, 96, 105–106;
    insects, 51
Edison, Thomas, 88, 90
Eelgrass, 65

Eggs, 31, 43, 103
Egypt, ancient, 78, 81, 83
Electric eel, 46
Electricity, 88
Elephants, 13–14, 26; White, 13
Emancipation Proclamation, 73 *See*
    Slavery.
Embalming: *See* Mummies.
Ericson, Leif, 69
Extinct species, 30, 37–38
Eyes: animal, 15, 19, 21, 33; human,
    115, 116

Fainting, 95
Fairytales, 78
Fasting, 94
Fingernails, 118
Fingerprinting, 90
Fireflies, 53
Fish: air-breathing, 43-44; biggest,
    47; drowning, 43; flying, 45; noisy,
    148; raining, 133; reproduction, 43
    See name of fish.
Flags, American, 72
Flies, 51, 53
Floods, 134
Flowers, 60, 62, 95–96
Flying: animals, 15, 22; birds, 30, 32,
    34; fish, 45
Foods, human; 59, 63, 101–107;
    calories in, 103; chewing, 96;
    digesting, 93; natural, 97; origins
    of, 64, 101, 102, 103, 104, 107;
    poisonous, 97, 105; spicy, 102;
    vitamins in, 104
Football, 124–125
Forest fires, 61
Fossils, 38, 83
Freckles, 116
French Foreign Legion, 84
Frostbite, 94
Fruits: chemicals in, 97; ripeness of,
    103, 104–105 *See* Bananas, Pine-
    apples, Trees.
Fulton, Robert, 89 *See* Steam engine.

Galileo, 87
Games, non-athletic, 123–124, 125, 127 *See* Sports.
Giants, human, 114
Glaciers, 142 *See* Icebergs.
Glass snakes, 40 *See* Lizards.
Goats, 15, 20–21
Gorillas, 11
Grapes, 62
Grass, 60
Gravity, 88, 152
Groundhog Day, 22 *See* Woodchucks.
Growing pains, 93
Growth, human, 93
Guillotine, 90
Guinea pigs, 25 *See* Rodents.
Gum, chewing, 62, 101

Hail, 133
Hair: cat, 19; human, 114-115; rhinoceros, 15
Handwriting, 82
Hares, 22
Hay fever, 95
Heart, 96
Herbs, 63
Himalayas, 17, 34, 140
Hippopotamuses, 17
Hog-nosed snakes, 41
Home runs, most, 121–122 *See* Baseball.
Honey, 53–54 *See* Bees.
Horns, 15
Horses, 25–26, 126
Horseshoe crabs, 46
Hudson, Hendrick, 79
Human beings; biggest eater, 105–106; oldest, 118 *See* Aging, Appetites, Bodies, Dreams, Eating, Foods, Growth, Illness, Intelligence, Men, Personality, Prehistoric, Senses, Teeth, Women.
Hummingbirds, 30, 105–106
Hurricanes, 132
Hyenas, 12, 26

Icebergs, 146–147 *See* Glaciers.
Ice cream, 93, 103
Illness, human, 93–97; cures for, 94, 95, 96
Indians, American, 71, 73–74, 75–76, 101
Insects, 51–56; non-eating, 51
Intelligence, human, 114

Joan of Arc, 79
Jujitsu, 122

Kangaroos, 12, 15
Ketchup, 102
Knights, medieval, 80
Koala bears, 12, 24

Lemmings, 16
Liberty Bell, 71
Lightbulbs, 88
Lightning, 132
Lincoln, Abraham, 73
Lions, 11, 12–13
Lizards, 14, 40, 41–42
Log cabins, 74–75
Loons, 32

Magellan, 83
Mammals, 11–26; color blindness in, 21; flying, 15–16, 21 *See* Animals.
Man: *See* Human beings.
Maples, tapping, 62
Marco Polo, 102
Marine plants, 63, 65
Marsupials, 12, 24 *See* Opossums, Koala Bears, Kangaroos.
Mating, animal, 26, 29
Mayflower: landing, 76; passengers, 72
Men, 115, 117
Meteors: *See* Shooting stars.
Mexican jumping beans, 52–53
Mice, 13, 19, 20
Milk, 40, 97–98, 101, 102
Milk snakes, 40

Millipedes, 54
Mirages, 141
Moles, 21
Monkeys, 11, 17
Moon, 152, 153
Mosquitoes, 51, 52
Mother Goose, 78
Moths, 52 *See* Caterpillars.
Mountains, highest, 140, 147
Mummies, 83
Muscles, human, 114, 115, 116, 118

Nazis, 82
Nero, 79, 80, 103 *See* Rome.
Newton, Sir Isaac, 88
Night vision, 15, 19, 33
North Pole, 33, 131 *See* Arctic.
Novas, 151 *See* Stars.
Numbers, Arabic, 87
Nuts, 59

Oceans, 140, 145, 146–149
Octopus, 43
Olympics, 126
Opossum, 12, 17–18
Orchids, 62
Organic foods: *See* Foods.
Ostriches, 30–31
Owls, 33
Oxygen, 95–96
Oysters, 104, 105

Palmistry, 111–112
Pasteurizing, 106 *See* Milk.
Peanuts, 59
Pearls, 104
Penguins, 29, 30, 33
Pennsylvania Dutch, 73
People: *See* Human beings.
Personality, 111–112
Phonograph, 90
Pigs, 21, 25, 125
Pilgrims, 72, 74, 76
Pineapples, 64
Ping-Pong, 122

Plants, 59–65; growing under ice, 65; man-eating, 59; medicinal, 65
Plymouth, Mass., colony of, 72–73, 75, 76
Pocahontas, 73–74, 83
Polo, 126
Porcupines, 18
Pouches, animals with, 12, 24 *See* Marsupials.
Prairie dogs, 20, 24
Prehistoric man, 38
Printing, development of, 82
Puritans, 74, 76

Quicklime, 142

Rabbits, 21, 22
Rabies, 16, 94
Raccoons, 17, 24, 94
Rain, 131, 133, 134, 135
Raleigh, Sir Walter, 81, 83
Rattlesnakes, 40
Redwoods, 61
Religion, 82
Reproduction: by birds, 29, 31; by humans, 97; by mammals, 14–15, 26
Revere, Paul, 69–70
Robins, 33, 105
Rockets, 153
Rodents, 20, 39, 40 *See* Capybara, Mice, Squirrels, Woodchucks.
Rome, ancient, 78, 79, 81, 84, 126
Ross, Betsy, 72
Ruth, Babe, 121–122

Sand, 30, 31, 141; -storms, 134
Sandwiches, 104
Sap, tree, 62
Sardines, 106
Sargasso Sea, 147
Scalping, 75–76
Scarecrows, 32
Scavengers, 12–13
Seashells, 150

Seaweed, 65, 147
Senses, human, 113, 116
Seven, mystic numeral, 115
Sex, dominant, 26
Sharks, 43; man-eating, 45
Sheep, 15, 126
Shooting stars, 151
Signatures, 82
Skunks, 18, 94
Sky, color of, 152
Slavery, 71, 73
Sleeping: by animals, 18, 25; by
    birds, 29; by humans, 113
Sleet, 131
Smiling, 118
Smith, Captain John, 73–74
Snakes, 38–41; eating habits, 39, 40;
    poisonous, 38, 39, 40, 95
Snow, 131, 143
Soda, 101
Sound, speed of, 148
South Pole, 33, 93, 131 *See* Antarctica.
Space travel, 153
Spiders, 55, 56, 96; webs of, 55
Sponges, 63–64
Sports, 121–127
Squirrels, 20, 22, 24, 94; flying, 22, 23
Stars, 149, 150–151, 152
Steamboats, 89
Steam engines, 88, 89
Sugar, 62, 94
Suicide, by animals, 16
Sun, 96, 152 *See* Stars.
Sunburns, 96
Surfing, 125
Swamps, 143
Swastika, 82

Tails, 14, 18, 40
Tarantulas, 56
Taste, sense of, 102, 116
Tears, 116

Teeth, 95, 96
Telescope, 149–151; invention of, 87
Tell, William, 83
Tennis, 125, 126
Tidal waves, 145
Tides, 145, 152
Toads, 41; horned, 41–42
Tobacco, 83
Tool making, 11
Top spinning, 123–124
Trees, 61–62, 63; apple, 77
Tulips, 60

UFOs, 154
Undertows, 148
Universe: *See* Stars, Sun, Earth,
    Moon.

Vanilla, 62
Viruses, 93
Volcanoes, 140, 145

Washington, George, 70, 72, 73, 75
Wasps, 26, 53
Water, fresh, 14, 16, 61, 63, 93, 102,
    143, 144, 148 *See* Oceans.
Watt, James, 88 *See* Steam engines.
Weather, 131–135; coldest, 131;
    desert, 135; forecasting, 22, 24, 32;
    tropical, 131
Weeds, 59, 65
Whales, 37, 46, 47
Whiskey, 95
White elephants, 13 *See* Elephants.
White House, 75
Wine, 62, 98
Witchcraft, 76 77, 79, 84
Women, 97, 117
Woodchucks, 20, 22, 94
Worms, 33, 54–55

Yo-yo, 127

ABOUT THE AUTHORS

Rhoda Blumberg has written many books for children on a wide variety of subjects. They include: *Southern Africa, Firefighters, Famine, UFOs, First Ladies, Sharks, The First Travel Guide to the Moon* and *The First Travel Guide to the Bottom of the Sea.*

Her daughter, Leda Blumberg, is the author of *Pets,* and she is currently preparing *The Complete Book of Horses* for Wanderer Books.